A PLEA FOR EMIGRATION

A PLEA FOR EMIGRATION;
OR NOTES OF CANADA WEST

Mary Ann Shadd

a *Broadview Anthology of British Literature* edition

Advisory Editor, *A Plea for Emigration*
Phanuel Antwi, University of British Columbia

General Editors,
The Broadview Anthology of British Literature:
Joseph Black, University of Massachusetts, Amherst
Leonard Conolly, Trent University
Kate Flint, University of Southern California
Isobel Grundy, University of Alberta
Don LePan, Broadview Press
Roy Liuzza, University of Tennessee
Jerome J. McGann, University of Virginia
Anne Lake Prescott, Barnard College
Barry V. Qualls, Rutgers University
Claire Waters, University of California, Davis

broadview press

BROADVIEW PRESS – www.broadviewpress.com
Peterborough, Ontario, Canada

Founded in 1985, Broadview Press remains a wholly independent publishing house. Broadview's focus is on academic publishing: our titles are accessible to university and college students as well as scholars and general readers. With over 600 titles in print, Broadview has become a leading international publisher in the humanities, with world-wide distribution. Broadview is committed to environmentally responsible publishing and fair business practices.

The interior of this book is printed on 100% recycled paper.

Library and Archives Canada Cataloguing in Publication

Shadd, Mary A., 1823-1893
[Plea for emigration]
    A plea for emigration; or, Notes of Canada West / Mary Ann Shadd ; advisory editor, A plea for emigration, Phanuel Antwi, University of British Columbia.

(A Broadview anthology of British literature edition)
Includes bibliographical references.
ISBN 978-1-55481-321-6 (paperback)

    1. Immigrants—Ontario—Guidebooks. 2. Blacks—Travel—Ontario—Guidebooks. 3. Ontario—Guidebooks. 4. Ontario—Description and travel. 5. Ontario—Social conditions—19th century. 6. Ontario—Emigration and immigration. I. Antwi, Phanuel, editor II. Title. III. Title: Notes of Canada West. IV. Title: Plea for emigration. V. Title: Shadd, Mary A., 1823-1893 . Plea for emigration VI. Series: Broadview anthology of British literature (Series)

FC3085.1.S52 2016   971.3'00496   C2016-904427-0

Broadview Press handles its own distribution in North America
PO Box 1243, Peterborough, Ontario, Canada K9J 7H5, Canada
555 Riverwalk Parkway, Tonawanda, NY 14150, USA
Tel: (705) 743-8990; Fax: (705) 743-8353
email: customerservice@broadviewpress.com

Distribution is handled by Eurospan Group in the UK, Europe, Central Asia, Middle East, Africa, India, Southeast Asia, Central America, and the Caribbean. Distribution is handled by Footprint Books in Australia and New Zealand.

Broadview Press acknowledges the financial support of the Government of Canada through the Canada Book Fund for our publishing activities.   Canada

Developmental Editors: Laura Buzzard, John Geddert, Jennifer McCue
Cover Designer: Lisa Brawn
Typesetter: Alexandria Stuart

PRINTED IN CANADA

Contents

Introduction

Mary Ann Shadd

1823 – 1893

Though she is relatively unknown, Mary Ann Shadd was a figure of real importance to mid nineteenth-century American and Canadian history. As founder and editor of the *Provincial Freeman and Daily Advertiser*, she has the distinction of being the first woman to start a newspaper in Canada, as well as the first black woman newspaper editor in North America. Later in life she attended Howard University School of Law—and became as influential a figure in the women's rights movement as she had been earlier in her life as a leader in Canadian and American black communities. As an educator, Shadd worked tirelessly to improve conditions for black children, and founded several schools; she also worked to educate people who had been freed from slavery or had escaped slavery. As an abolitionist, Shadd was particularly active in both Canada and the United States during the decade prior to the American Civil War, and she played an important role in encouraging the emigration of black people into Canada.

Shadd grew up in a family of free blacks in the slave state of Delaware. "Freedom," however, for black citizens of Delaware was a relative term; even free blacks were subject to widespread persecution during this era, throughout the United States and (arguably to a somewhat lesser extent) in Canada. Her father, Abraham Shadd, a shoemaker with shops in both Wilmington, Delaware, and West Chester, Pennsylvania, used the family home as a refuge for fugitive slaves, and was a representative for the state of Delaware at conventions for the Improvement of Free People of Color; later, he became the first black to hold elected office in British North America when, in 1859, he won a seat on the Raleigh Town Council. A similar determination to improve the situation of her people became a powerful force in Mary Shadd's own life. At the age of 16, after completing her education at a Quaker school for free blacks in West Chester, Shadd went on to form her own school in Wilmington. She soon became active more widely in the issues of the day; in the late 1840s her letters were published and her work discussed in the pages of Frederick Douglass's newspaper, the *North Star*.

With the passage of the Fugitive Slave Act of 1850, life became increasingly hazardous for free blacks (see below). Largely in order to avoid the risk of enslavement, Shadd's family joined the exodus into what was then Canada West.[1] Shadd saw the need for the education of escaped slaves in Canada, and soon opened up a school in Windsor with the financial support of the American Mission Association. She was also an advocate for emigration to Canada as a strategy of opposition to the oppression of blacks in the United States—an issue on which the black community was divided. Shadd put forward her case in an 1852 pamphlet "for the information of colored immigrants" entitled *A Plea for Emigration; or Notes of Canada West*.

Shadd's founding of the *Provincial Freeman* in 1853 (initially under the name of journalist Samuel Ringgold Ward to conceal its female authorship) provided her with another platform for putting forward her views—not only in favor of abolition, but also on education, on the role of women in society, on temperance (which she strongly supported), and against "exclusivity" (segregation, as it is termed today). As a staunch integrationist, Shadd was at odds with the segregationist leanings of some other abolitionists and activists of the era. In particular, she clashed with the well-known activist Henry Bibb (1815–54), editor of the newspaper *Voice of the Fugitive* and director of the Refugee Home Society, a settlement intended exclusively for freed slaves. Their disagreements—over the issue of exclusivity, various concerns relating to education, and what Shadd considered to be Bibb's unethical financial practices—ultimately led to the American Mission Association pulling funding from her school. Shadd gave lectures around the U.S. in order to raise funds for the school;

---

1   What is now Southern Ontario was the British Colony of Upper Canada from 1791 until 1841. (What is now the southern half of Quebec was during that period the British colony of Lower Canada—"lower" because it was downstream on the St Lawrence River from the upper reaches of that river and from the other rivers and lakes that flow into it.) In 1841 Upper and Lower Canada together became the United Province of Canada, and from that time until 1867 what is now Southern Ontario was known as Canada West. Only with Confederation in 1867 did the provinces of Ontario and Quebec come into existence.

she eventually relocated to Toronto, from where she continued for some years to edit the *Provincial Freeman*.

In 1856 Shadd married Toronto barber Thomas Cary, with whom she would have two children before his death in 1860. The *Freeman*, which had always struggled financially, folded in 1857, after being turned over to Mary's brother Isaac. (As had been the case when she founded it, there was resistance to the notion of a woman running a newspaper; her brother, however, turned out to be no better able to make a financial success of the paper.)

Like many who came to Canada through the "Underground Railroad," Shadd returned to the United States with the Emancipation Proclamation and the end of slavery. She assisted in the recruitment of black soldiers, and later worked in the education and settlement of emancipated slaves. After teaching in Detroit and Washington, D.C., Shadd entered Howard University Law School in 1868; in 1883 she completed her degree, becoming the second black woman to earn a law degree in the United States.

In the 1870s and 1880s Shadd became increasingly active in the suffrage movement (and in the movement regarding women's rights more generally); her work was recognized by, among others, Elizabeth Cady Stanton (arguably the leading figure in the suffrage movement in America). Shadd remained active as a writer for various newspapers, and continued to work to improve the lives of African Americans (including, in the 1870s, as an agent for Frederick Douglass's newspaper, the *New National Era*).

Shadd died in Washington in 1893. Until her death she continued to teach and to promote the causes of women's rights and black education.

A Plea for Emigration

A *Plea for Emigration* holds an unusual place in literary history. From one angle it may be said to belong to a genre of writing that became widespread in the eighteenth century and continued throughout much of the nineteenth: the settler guide, designed to inform prospective immigrants of conditions in one part or another of North America. The authors of many of these publications were glowing in their depiction of life in the New World—and economical with the truth, downplaying such things as the realities of winter in northern North America. (Such is the case with some of the materials Shadd quotes from in her work; it is very much the case as well with the description of Canada in *Smith's Canadian Gazetteer* [1846], included as part of the "In Context" materials below.) A parallel tradition took a very different tone, painting a far less rosy picture of life in the colonies, and aiming to dampen the "vain expectations raised in the minds of such credulous persons as seek superior comfort and felicity on the continent of America" (as an anonymous 1796 publication entitled *Look Before You Leap*[1] expressed it). The authors of both sorts of depiction of life in North America tended to be interested parties—some committed to increasing emigration (and often hoping in one way or another to benefit by it), others committed to trying to check emigration, often out of a concern that Britain was losing its skilled laborers to the enticing possibilities of the New World.

Shadd's *Plea for Emigration* differs in important respects from these and most other works addressed to potential emigrants. Whereas most such works were addressed to potential white emigrants to North America from Britain or continental Europe, Shadd's aimed to entice black Americans to emigrate to Canada; Shadd's work is explicitly intended "for the information of colored immigrants."

If *A Plea for Emigration* deserves a place of note in this centuries-long tradition of emigration literature, it is at least as important to place the work in the context of the history of slavery and abolitionism. From the time of the Declaration of Independence, the issue of slavery was highly controversial in the United States. It became even more so in the 1780s and 1790s as slavery became more entrenched in Southern states while the Northern states all either abolished slavery outright or put in place measures that would lead to its gradual disappearance. How then to deal with slaves who escaped from Southern states to Northern ones? The Fugitive Slave Act of 1793 specified that it was an offense not only to try to escape slavery but also to assist others to do so; that a judge or magistrate could decide the status of those alleged to be fugitive slaves—and if the allegations were deemed to be true, enforce their return to slavery. It was not only

---

1   Catharine Parr-Traill's *The Backwoods of Canada* (1836) and Susannah Moodie's *Roughing It in the Bush* (1852) are the two best-known Canadian examples of work that connects with this latter tradition.

escaped slaves who were put in danger by the provisions of the Act; many free blacks—both in Southern states and in Northern ones—were kidnapped by slave hunters confident of being able to find a judge willing to accept almost any sworn testimony by whites as to the slave status of those they had captured. The Act, however, was strongly opposed by many Northerners, and in the late eighteenth and early nineteenth centuries several northern states put into place laws designed to undermine the federal law by, for example, requiring jury trials before alleged slaves could be placed in the custody of slave owners.

During the same period free individuals (both black and white) began in increasing numbers to assist those seeking to escape slavery, and to convey them either to relative safety in cities such as Boston with strong anti-slavery traditions, or to greater safety across the border in Canada. The loose network formed with this purpose came in due course to be known as the Underground Railroad. Since its activities were illegal, euphemisms were widely used: escaped slaves were "passengers," someone facilitating their movement north was a "conductor," Detroit (the point from which many left the United States) was "Midnight"; journey's end on the Canadian side was "Dawn." (In time, an actual community named Dawn grew up east of Windsor, Ontario.)

On the Canadian side the situation for black immigrants from the United States was in many respects analogous to that in the Northern states; slavery had existed in all the British colonies that eventually became Canada, but a series of legal decisions and new pieces of legislation in the 1780s and 1790s in the various colonies either prohibited slavery outright, or provided for its gradual abolition. Change occurred at different rates in the different colonies of what is now Canada, but with the enactment in 1834 of the 1833 Slavery Abolition Act of the British Parliament, slavery was officially ended in all the Canadian colonies, as it was throughout the British Empire.

Many in the southern States had long protested that the provisions of the 1793 Fugitive Slave Act were too weak; the issue became entangled with other issues relating to whether slavery would be allowed in the territories America had acquired from Mexico during the Mexican-American War of 1846 to 48. Under the provisions of the "Compromise of 1850" California would enter the union as a free state (i.e., one in which slavery was illegal), special arrangements would be made regarding Utah and New Mexico, and the provisions of the Fugitive Slave Act would be strengthened. In accordance with this "compromise," Congress passed a new Fugitive Slave Act (see the "In Context" materials below), which specified that no "alleged fugitive" would be allowed to testify in his or her own defense, and which substantially increased the penalties for those found to have assisted fugitives. In the face of the increased danger posed by the new Act, passenger traffic on the underground railroad also increased—as did controversy over the Act's provisions, and, more generally, concern about how best to respond to the institution of slavery. Among black North Americans, controversy took several forms. One was over the sorts of collective responsibility blacks might bear, and whether or not such responsibilities were to themselves or "to be seen and admired by the whites," as Shadd put it in her controversial "Hints to the Colored People of the North" (1849). Another was over the degree to which blacks should aim for "exclusivity"—what later came to be called segregation—or aim to mix with white society; what were the dangers of "assimilation"?

A related controversy was over how best to resist the evils of slavery. The escaped slave and leading abolitionist Frederick Douglass was among those who did not support efforts to assist the emigration of black Americans via the Underground Railroad; it was important, he felt, for blacks to protest slavery and make their claims to equal rights as Americans, by remaining in the country (see the "In Context" materials below). Like Douglass, Shadd was an opponent of "exclusivity." On the matter of emigration in the face of the threats posed by the 1850 Fugitive Slave Act, however, she parted company with the great abolitionist; it was in the context of this controversy that she published *A Plea for Emigration*.

In all this it is important to remain aware that when Shadd recommended that escaped slaves and "free colored people" emigrate from the United States to "Canada," the place she referred to was very different from the independent nation that we know as "Canada" today. The province of Canada was a colonial territory within the British Empire; the areas in which it could exercise independent control over its own affairs were quite limited. To Shadd, it was a large part of the attraction of Canada as a destination that emigrants to Canada would be "under British protection." Shadd sees other British colonies in the same light; it is a powerful argument for moving to Jamaica and other British colonies in the West Indies that there, too, emigrants would be under the protection of British laws. What government, she asks rhetorically, is "so powerful and so thoroughly impartial, ... so practically anti-slavery, and so protective," as Her Majesty's? In like fashion she recommends "Vancouver's Island"—at that time a British colony quite unconnected to the province of "Canada"—in large part because it is "under the protection of Great Britain." It is sometimes assumed that colonialism and freedom operate always in uncomplicated opposition to each other. Shadd's writings—her articles in the *Provincial Freeman* and elsewhere as well as her *Plea for Emigration*—remind us of just how complex such connections could be in the three decades that elapsed between slavery's abolition in Britain and its colonies,[1] and its abolition in the United States.

A Note on the Text

The present text has been transcribed for *The Broadview Anthology of British Literature* from the 1852 facsimile of the one copy extant, which has been made available through the Early Canadiana Online database (and is sufficiently worn at the corners of many pages as to be barely legible). Punctuation has in the present version been modernized; some obvious errors have been silently corrected; and very occasional changes have been made to the paragraph breaks in the original. The American spelling of the original (printed in Detroit by George W. Pattison) has been retained. Richard Almonte's 1998 edition, which adopts Canadian spelling and substantially alters Shadd's paragraph breaks as well as her punctuation, has also been extensively consulted.

---

1   An Act for the Abolition of Slavery throughout the British Colonies (1833) exempted "territories in the possession of the East India Company," which, although under British control, were not technically colonies; in those territories slavery was not abolished for another decade.

A PLEA FOR EMIGRATION;
OR NOTES OF CANADA WEST

A PLEA FOR EMIGRATION:

OR,

NOTES OF CANADA WEST,

IN ITS

MORAL, SOCIAL, AND POLITICAL ASPECT:

WITH

SUGGESTIONS RESPECTING MEXICO, WEST INDIES, AND VANCOUVER'S ISLAND,

FOR THE

INFORMATION OF COLORED EMIGRANTS.

BY MARY A. SHADD.

DETROIT:
PRINTED BY GEORGE W. PATTISON.
1852.

Title page of *A Plea for Emigration*
in its original 1852 pamphlet form.

INTRODUCTORY REMARKS

The increasing desire on the part of the colored people to become thoroughly informed respecting the Canadas, and particularly that part of the province called Canada West[1]—to learn of the climate, soil, and production, and of the inducements offered generally to emigrants, and to them particularly, since that the passage of the odious Fugitive Slave Law[2] has made a residence in the United States to many of them dangerous in the extreme—this consideration, and the absence of condensed information accessible to all, is my excuse for offering this tract to the notice of the public.

The people are in a strait.[3] On the one hand, a pro-slavery administration, with its entire controllable force, is bearing upon them with fatal effect: on the other, the Colonization Society,[4] in the Garb of *Christianity* and *Philanthropy*, is seconding the efforts of the first named power, by bringing into the lists a vast social and immoral influence, thus making more effective the agencies employed. Information is needed. Tropical Africa, the land of promise of the colonizationists, teeming as she is with breath of pestilence, a burning sun, and fearful maladies, bids them welcome; she feelingly invites [them] to moral and physical death, under a voluntary escort of their most bitter enemies at home. Again, many look with dreadful forebodings to the probability of worse than inquisitorial inhumanity in the Southern States from the operation of the Fugitive Law. Certain that neither a home in Africa, nor in the Southern States, is desireable under present circumstances, inquiry is made respecting

---

1 *Canadas ... Canada West* Prior to 1841 the provinces of Upper and Lower Canada were independent political entities. After British Parliament passed the Act of Union in 1840 they became one single province, divided into the administrative districts of Canada West and Canada East, which correspond with present-day Ontario and Quebec.

2 *Fugitive Slave Law* Enacted by U.S. Congress in 1850, this law mandated the hiring of officials and issuing of warrants for hunting down and arresting fugitive slaves. $10 rewards were given for the return of slaves, and $5 for the capture of freed blacks. Penalties for hindering this process were substantially increased.

3 *strait* Dilemma.

4 *Colonization Society* The American Society for Colonizing the Free People of Color of the United States, an organization of white Americans that encouraged the emigration of blacks from America to Africa; it was under the auspices of the Society that a settlement for former American slaves was established in Liberia, in West Africa.

Canada. I have endeavored to furnish information to a certain extent, to that end, and believing that more reliance would be placed upon a statement of facts obtained in that country, from reliable sources and from observation, than upon a repetition of current statements made elsewhere, however honestly made, I determined to visit Canada, and to there collect such information as most persons desire. These pages contain the result of much inquiry—matter obtained both from individuals and from documents and papers of unquestionable character in the province.

A Plea for Emigration, & c.

British America

British America, it is well known, is a country equal in extent, at least, to the United States, extending on the north to the Arctic Ocean, from the Atlantic on the east, to the Pacific on the west, and the southern boundary of which is subject to the inequalities in latitude of the several Northern States and Territories[1] belonging to the United States government. This vast country includes within its limits, some of the most beautiful lakes and rivers on the Western Continent. The climate, in the higher latitudes, is extremely severe, but for a considerable distance north of the settled districts, particularly in the western part, the climate is healthy and temperate: epidemics are not of such frequency as in the United Sates, owing to a more equable temperature, and local diseases are unknown. The province claiming especial attention, as presenting features most desirable in a residence, is Canada, divided into East and West; and of these Canada West is to be preferred.

The Canadas—Climate Etc.

Canada East, from geographical position and natural characteristics, is not so well suited to a variety of pursuits, as the more western part of the province. The surface is generally uneven, and in many

---

1   *Northern States and Territories* Refers to the Oregon Territory, the Minnesota Territory, and the Unorganized Territory that lay in between the two.

parts mountainous; its more northern location subject the inhabitants to extremely cold, cheerless winters, and short but warm summers. The land is of good quality, and vegetation is of rapid growth, but the general healthiness of the country is inferior to some of the other districts. The State of Maine presents a fair sample of Lower Canada in general. Population (which is principally French) is confined chiefly to the valley of the St. Lawrence, and the country contiguous.[1] In Canada West, the variation from salubrious[2] and eminently healthy climate, is nowhere sufficient to cause the least solicitude;[3] on the contrary, exempt from the steady and enfeebling warmth of southern latitudes, and the equally injurious characteristics of polar countries, it is highly conducive to mental and physical energy. Persons living in the vicinity of the Great Lakes, and the neighboring districts, say that their winters are much less severe than when, the past years, vast forests covered that region—that very deep snows are less frequent than they were, and that owing to the great body of ice that accumulates in the Lakes, the people living in the States bordering, suffer more severely from the cold than Canadians:—the ice making more intense the north winds sweeping over it. If these statements admit of a doubt, we well know that many flourishing towns in Canada are farther south than a large portion of Maine, New Hampshire, Vermont, New York, Michigan and Oregon, and should, in considering this fact, have the full benefit of geographical position. I have thought proper to allude to the cold, at first, for the reason that it is the feature in the climate most dwelt upon—the solicitude of friends, ignorant on this point, and of person less disinterested, often appealing to fears having no foundation whatever, when the facts are fairly set forth.

The products of a country make an important item, in all cases in which this question is being considered; so in the present instance. In Canada we find the vegetation of as rank[4] growth as in the middle and northern United States. In order to promote a luxuriance in the products of a country equally with another, the conditions necessary to that end must be equal,—if by reference to facts, an approach to similarity can be made, that part of the subject will be settled for the

---

1 *contiguous* Touching; sharing a common border.
2 *salubrious* Health-giving.
3 *solicitude* Concern.
4 *rank* Thick and abundant.

present. As early as March there are indications of permanent Spring weather and in June and July, the summer will compare with the same season south of the line. In January and February there are always cold spells and warm alternating, as in our experiences; but when the warm season commences, the heat is intense, and the growth of vegetation is rapid, so that whatever deficiency may be attributed to a brief period, may be fully compensated for in the steady and equal temperature after the warm season has fairly set in; though it is late beginning, it is prolonged into what is the autumn with us, and farmers harvest their crops of wheat, hay, &c, at a later period than in the Middle States, generally,—August and September being the months in which hay, wheat, and some other crops are gathered in. Taking this circumstance in connection with the regularity of the seasons, and uniform heat or cold when they have such weather, the superiority of many products, as wheat, fruit, &c., may be accounted for. I say superiority, because, in its place, I hope to give such evidence as will substantiate the assertion. Annexed is a table setting forth the greatest degree of cold and heat,—in the years mentioned, as indicated by Fahrenheit's Thermometer, together with the highest and lowest range indicated in the months of September and December of 1851, which last has been said to be unusual, (the lowest in twenty years) by the "oldest inhabitant."

	Greatest Deg. of Heat	Lowest Deg. of Cold
1840	82.4°	18.6°
1841	93.1°	6.7°
1842	91°	1.9°
1843	89°	9.4°
1844	86.8°	7.2°
1845	95°	4.2°
1846	94.6°	16.7°
1847	87°	2.9°

"These are the extreme ranges of cold and heat indicated at the Observatory, on one day during the seasons, but which do not last beyond a few hours; the main temperature of the four months of summer and four of winter for the last eight years have been relatively:

Summer 75. 6°, Winter 26.7°, Fahrenheit."[1] In addition to the usual state of the weather of the last year as contrasted with former period, the last summer and first autumn month were very warm, and in the month of September indicated 95° Fahrenheit, in the shade, without eliciting remarks other than a similar state of weather, at that season, would have in the United States. In short, from much conversation with persons of many years residence, I believe that climate opposes no obstacle to emigration, but that it is most desirable known in so high a latitude, for emigrants generally, and colored people particularly. In other parts of British America, as for instance, Lower Canada, Nova Scotia and New Britain,[2] the cold is more intense, but when we think of the extent of Upper Canada, there would be no more reason for ascribing severe cold to the whole, than there would be to class the climate of the United States with that of the torrid zone, because of the great heat in the lower latitudes. In this province the regularity of the season promote health in a greater degree than in those countries subject to frequent changes, as in many of the United States, where cold and warm weather alternate in quick succession; and in the upper province especially, universal testimony to the healthiness of the climate obtains.

SOILS—TIMBER—CLEARING LANDS

The quality and different kinds of soil must form the second subject for consideration, because, in connection with climate, it enters largely into all our ideas of comfort and pecuniary[3] independence: again, because so far as colored people are interested in the subject of emigration to any country, their welfare in a pecuniary view, is promoted by attention to the quality of the soil. Lands out of the United States, on this continent, should have no local value, if the question of personal freedom and political rights were left out of the

---

1   *GREATEST DEG. … Fahrenheit* As Richard Almonte notes in his edition of Shadd's work, Shadd is quoting here from an 1848 pamphlet entitled *Catechism of Information for Intended Emigrants of All Classes to Upper Canada*, which she evidently used frequently for reference material in writing *A Plea for Emigration.*
2   *New Britain* Likely New Brunswick.
3   *pecuniary* Monetary; financial.

subject, but as they are paramount, too much may not be said on this point. I mean to be understood, that a description of lands in Mexico would probably be as desirable as lands in Canada, if the idea were simply to get lands and settle thereon; but it is important to know if by this investigation we only agitate and leave the public mind in an unsettled state, or if a permanent nationality is included in the prospect of becoming purchasers and settlers.

The question *does the soil of Canada offer inducements sufficient to determine prospective emigrants in its favor?* may be answered by everyone himself, after having properly weighed the following facts. Persons who have been engaged in agriculture the greater part of their lives—practical and competent farmers, and judges of the capacity of different soils—say that the soil is unsurpassed by that of Kentucky and States farther south, and naturally superior to the adjoining northern States. It is not only indicated by the rich dark and heavy appearance, and the depth of the soil, which is seldom reached by plows of the greatest capacity, but by the character of the products, and the unequalled growth and size of timber on un-cleared lands. Wheat, the staple product of the country, averages sixty pounds to the bushel—often actually exceeding that; fifty-six is the standard weight in the United States; and leaving out Delaware, that is seldom reached. The forest consists of walnut, hickory, white and burr oak, basswood, ash, pine, poplar—all of the largest size, and other inferior kinds of woods with which we are familiar in our northern woods. There is a greater variety in them, and larger size, and knowing that the size of vegetables depends mainly upon the quantity of nutriment[1] afforded by the soil, we are led in this instance to infer its superiority. Besides the well known wheat, oats, buckwheat, Indian corn, and other grains, are raised of good quality, and with profit, and more to the *acre* than is usually obtained in the States, except on the application of fertilizing materials—a mode not much practised in Canada hitherto, the land not having been exhausted sufficiently to require such appliances to further its productiveness. The varieties of soil, are a black loam, sandy loam, clay, and sand, but a black loam is the predominating kind. I speak now of the cultivated districts, and

---

1 *nutriment* Nourishment; sustenance.

those in process of clearing, as far north as Lord Selkirk's settlement,[1] for the country beyond the present limits of civilization, I do not feel warranted in speaking, nor to give in other than general terms, the testimony of those acquainted with that region. It is said to be equally fertile, but the products not so varied, because of its more northern situation. The general appearance of the province is undulating,[2] though there is much level country. Numerous and beautiful rivers, and smaller streams, run through the country, in all directions, so there is no lack of water power. "The plains," a term applied to level country, "are generally sandy, and yield regular average and certain crops, without reference to the season."[3] They are similar to the western prairies, but more capital is necessary to cultivate them for timber lands. The advantage of timberland, to purchasers of small capital, over plains, is considerable. On cultivated, or plain lands, on which timber is thinly scattered, the earliest return for labor spent is deferred to the growth of the crop; besides the mode of tillage is different. Not so on the timbered lands; wood ever meets a ready and cash sale, and more may be realized from firewood than to three times pay the cost of a farm. Woodland will average seventy cords to the acre, every cord of which can be readily disposed of at two and a half dollars,[4] cash, in the towns. The regularity of the seasons tends, also, to increase the farmer's security, so that all other men, he is least apprehensive of want. "If the fall wheat fails," says the little book referred to, "he replaces it with spring wheat; and our seasons are so peculiar that some crops are always certain to be productive." ... Those whose capital invested in it is their own, are sure to increase their means and wealth.... "If a farmer determines to keep out of debt, and be satisfied with what his farm yields, independence in a few years will be the result."[5] The above extracts are intended for the benefit of the emigrants in general—men of small means or with no capital—and

---

1 *Lord Selkirk's settlement* The Red River Settlement, a colony of Scottish Highlanders and Irishmen located in what is now Manitoba. It was founded by Thomas Douglas, 5th Earl of Selkirk (1771–1820) in 1811.

2 *undulating* Hilly.

3 *The plains ... the season* As Almonte has pointed out, Shadd is again here quoting from *Catechism of Information for Intended Emigrants of All Classes to Upper Canada*.

4 *two and a half dollars* Refers to U.S. Dollars.

5 *If the fall ... result* From *Catechism of Information for Intended Emigrants of All Classes to Upper Canada*.

show what may be expected by generally the least wealthy who settle in a new county.

From the many instances of success under my observation, (particularly of formerly totally destitute colored persons) I firmly believe that with an axe and a little energy, an independent position would result in a short period. The cost of clearing wild lands, is also an important item; by that is meant putting land in a state to receive a crop,—it includes clearing of trees, fencing etc. This can be done at less cost near the settled districts. "In moderately timbered" lands, ten dollars the acre is the least for which it can be done,—more remote, the price varies from that to twenty dollars. Though the prevalent opinion in the province, is, that the soil is second to none for agricultural purposes, yet it is hardly possible to state the actual productiveness of the soil, as the attention has not been given to farming that the land admits. There are, and must be for a time, few experimental and scientific farmers, as it is more as a means of present subsistence, than to test the capacity of different soils that the farmer labors to procure a crop; though the conviction is irresistible that indigence[1] and moderate competence must at no distant day, give place to wealth, intelligence, and their concomitants.[2]

GRAINS, POTATOES, TURNIPS, &C.

The accompanying table exhibits the average yield to the acre, of the several grains mentioned, in fallow[3] land:

ARTICLES	No. BUSH	ARTICLES	No. BUSH
Wheat, – – – – –	30	Oats, – – – – –	70
Buckwheat, – – – –	15	Barley, – – – – –	40
Rye, – – – – –	35	Indian Corn, – – – –	50

Other products yielding a profitable return, and that form a part of the crop in well cultivated farms generally, in the United States are potatoes (white or Irish and sweet), carrots, turnips, pumpkins,

---

1 *indigence* Extreme poverty.
2 *concomitants* Associated qualities; those things which naturally accompany something.
3 *fallow* Plowed but left unsown.

(several kinds and the best I ever saw), squashes, and tobacco. These vegetables grow very large, and are not included in what we term garden plants. I have never seen in the large markets of our northern cities, vegetables of the class here mentioned, to equal them in the general, except the sweet potato. The Irish potato grows much larger, and is in every respect superior; so of the others. Tobacco grows finely, and meets with ready sale at what would be called a high price with us. These articles, I repeat are of the finest description, and have not, of course, the pithy[1] and stringy characteristics so general in the same kind with us. It is difficult to get at the average yield of such things, except potatoes and turnips, but a full crop will convey the idea.

The most abundant are tomatoes, cucumbers, onions, beets, cabbage and cauliflower, egg-plants, beans, peas, leeks, celery, lettuce, asparagus, melons, (water-melons and musk-melons,) cantaloupes and spinach. There are other vegetables, but they have been mentioned elsewhere. These articles, excepting water-melons and cantaloupes, are cultivated with as great success, at least, as in the United States, and the specimens generally seen in the gardens and market-places are decidedly superior.

FRUITS—VINES—BERRIES

Canada is emphatically a fruit country. The fruits of New York, Michigan and New Jersey, have long been famous: but if comparison is fairly instituted, pre-eminence will be the award to the Province. Apples grow in abundance, wild and cultivated, from the diminutive crab to the highly flavored bell-flower and pippin; and pears, plums, and cherries, in many varieties. The extent to which fruit is cultivated, and the yield, are incredible. Egg and blue plums are raised with ease, and strawberries, raspberries, grapes, whortleberries,[2] and in fact all of the fruits seen in our markets, are plentiful. Other ideas than those of a barren soil, and scarcity of products, are induced when visiting the market-places of Toronto, Hamilton, and other large towns. At Toronto, may be seen one of the best markets in

---

1   *pithy* Containing much spongy tissue.
2   *whortleberries* Bilberries, closely related to blueberries.

America in every way—the supplies furnished by the farmers of their own agricultural districts. At the State Fair, held in Detroit, Michigan, 1851, the first prizes for fruits, fowls, and cattle, were awarded to Canada farmers; so of the Fair held in Western New York during the same year.

DOMESTIC ANIMALS—FOWLS—GAME

In the general, the horses are not of that large size found in the Middle and Western States, but are of medium size, particularly those used by the French; yet, occasionally, one may see large horses among them and cattle, sheep, etc. also. The size of cattle seems not to affect their market value as beef and mutton, it being thought by epicures[1] to be of the best quality. I speak of the French in this connection, because it is well known, they form no inconsiderable part of the population. Among English, and other farmers, more attention is paid to improving stock. Competition is as spiritedly carried on as in the States; consequently cattle and horses of the finest kinds, as to size and repute, are owned by them. The Canadian pony, with them, gives place to the fine English draft and carriage horse, and Durham and other kine of celebrity[2] are justly appreciated. The pride of Canadian farmers, as shown in a fine selection of such animals, is not at all less than that of the "American" neighbors: as before said, the highest premiums given for superior cattle and sheep at Rochester and Detroit, in 1851, were received by Canada Farmers. To understand fully the resources of the Canadas in this particular, both as to quantity and quality, for labor or other purposes, a view of the well stocked farms, with their swarms of horses, oxen, cows, sheep and hogs, would well repay a visit to the country, to those skeptical on these points, or to see the excellent beef, mutton, veal and pork, exposed for sale—unsurpassed anywhere for quality and abundance. Prices vary as elsewhere, according to demand, but ordinarily they are:

---

1   *epicures* People who take particular pleasure in fine food.
2   *kine of celebrity* Well known sorts of cows.

Beef, – – – – ᐧ– 4 and 5 cents per pound
Mutton, – – – – 5 and 5 cents per pound
Veal, – – – – – 4 and 5 cents per pound
Pork, – – – – – 5 and 6 cents per pound[1]

Again, the butter and cheese derived directly from these animals must be, and are, superior, from the nature of the pasture and other food eaten: though, from the circumstances of recent settlement, means of disposal and abundance, matters in the housewife's department are not generally so thoroughly conducted as in more populous and older settled countries, where a competition of tastes and judgment in managing these articles and arranging for the market, is freely indulged. The comparative cost of keeping stock is little, the summer pastures affording ample for the season; in winter, many mark their horses, and turn them out in the woodlands, and open country, where they never fail of a supply of roots, and grasses. Numbers are seen in mid-winter, looking as well as those housed and fed. The snows protect the grasses, and from their peculiar length and frequency, animals subsist well on the matter they are thus enabled to get by removing them, and from the early growth of shrubs in the woods. The farms generally, have chickens, turkeys, geese, and other fowls, in great numbers; and they meet with a ready sale—prices are generally for poultry two shillings and two and six-pence[2] the pair, when in great plenty; eggs 10 cents and 12 ½ cents the dozen, and may be disposed of in any quantity to the traders without leaving the farm: numerous hucksters go in all directions through the country to purchase, to sell again in the large cities. In the winter, these articles, in common with vegetable and other commodities, are often sold at a rate that in the United States would be called high, the rapidly increasing population making the ordinary supply insufficient. Geese uniformly command two shillings; turkeys one dollar, domesticated or wild. There is an abundance of game, and turkeys meet with ready sale. Hunting is much the custom of all classes, and ducks, squirrels, (black) pigeons, deer, hares, quails, pheasants, and other game, are

---

1 [Shadd's note] Prices of meat are not uniform, as before said and owing to the increased demands prices have risen very recently, to the ordinary price in the States. That, of course, will not be the rate henceforth, but will be determined by the supply.

2 *shillings ... six-pence* Refers to the Canadian Pound, used as currency until 1858.

brought down in great numbers. Wild animals are not troublesome, though in remote districts, an occasional bear or wolf is seen: foxes also make depredations[1] at times, but not frequently.

PRICES OF LAND IN THE COUNTRY—CITY PROPERTY, &C.

The country in the vicinity of Toronto and to the eastward, being thickly settled, (farms being advertised "thirty miles on Yonge Street"), the price of property is, of course, very much higher than in the western districts. City property varies according to location. Two hundred dollars the foot, is the value of lots in good position in Toronto: in the suburbs very fine lots may be had at reasonable rates. Farms, at a few miles distant, range from thirty to fifty dollars the acre—fifty dollars being thought a fair price for the best quality of land with improvements. But in the western districts farms may be bought for one thousand dollars, superior in every way to farms near the city of Toronto that are held at five thousand. Improved lands near Chatham, London, Hamilton, and other towns west may be bought at prices varying from ten up to one hundred: at a few miles distant, uncleared lands belonging to Government may be had by paying one dollar, sixty-two cents, two, and two fifty, according to locality—well timbered and [provided with] water, near cultivated farms on the river and lake shore. Thousands of acres, of the very best land in the Province, are now in the market at [the] above prices, and either in the interior, or well situated as to prospect from the lakes, and near excellent markets. The land is laid out in what are called concessions, these concessions, or blocks, being sub-divided into lots. There is, therefore, a uniformity of appearance throughout the farms, and no contest about roads on individual property can result—the roads being designed to benefit equally contiguous property, and under jurisdiction of Government. One hundred acres is the smallest quantity to be had of Government, but individual holders sell in quantities to suit purchasers. Large quantities of land are held by individuals, though at a higher rate generally than that held by Government: and their titles are said to be often defective. In every respect, the preference

---

1   *depredations* Acts of plunder; thefts.

should be for purchases of Government. Land is cheaper, is well situated, and below a specified number of acres, may not be bought (a prohibition of advantage to many who would buy, as there is induced a spirit of enterprise and competition, and a sense of responsibility). Too many are now *independently* dragging along miserably, on the few acres (ten, twenty, or such a matter), bought at the high rates of individual holders, in a country in which the prices must, for a long time, require more land in process of culture, to afford a comfortable support. There is every inducement to buy near or in towns, as well as in the country, as land is cheap, business increasing with the steady increase of populations, no lack of employment at fair prices, and no complexional[1] or other qualification in existence.

LABOR—TRADES

In Canada, as in other recently settled countries, there is much to do, and comparatively few for the work. The numerous towns and villages springing up, and the great demand for timber and agricultural products, make labor of every kind plenty: all trades that are practiced in the United States, are there patronized by whomsoever carried on—no man's complexion affecting his business. If a colored man understands his business, he receives the public patronage the same as white man. He is not obliged to work a little better, and at a lower rate—there is no degraded class to identify him with, therefore every man's work stands or falls according to merit, not as in his color. Builders, and other tradesmen, of different complexions, work together on the same building and in the same shop, with perfect harmony, and often the proprietor of an establishment is colored, and the majority or all of the men employed are white. Businesses that in older communities have ceased to remunerate,[2] yield a larger percentage to the money invested.

The mineral resources of the Canadas not being developed, to any extent, for fuel wood is generally used, and a profitable trade in the commodity is carried on; and besides lumber for buildings, the getting out

---

1 *complexional* Based on complexion, skin color; i.e., there are no qualifications of race.
2 *remunerate* Pay for services done.

of materials for staves, coopers' stuff[1] and various purposes, affords steady employment and at fair prices for cash. This state of things must increase, and assume more importance in Canada markets, as the increasing population of the western United States burn and otherwise appropriate their timber. Railroads are in process of construction—steamboats now ply between Toronto and the several towns on the lakes; and in process of time, iron and other works will be in operation, it is said, all requiring their quota, and of course keeping up the demand. Boards for home and foreign markets, are successfully manufactured, and numerous mill-sites are fast being appropriated to saw and grist mills. In some sections, colored men are engaged in saw mills on their own account. At Dawn,[2] a settlement in the Sydenham, (of which hereafter,) and at other points, this trade is prosecuted with profit to them. To enumerate the different occupations in which colored persons are engaged, even in detail, would but fatigue, and would not further the end in view, namely: To set forth the advantage of a residence in a country, in which chattel slavery[3] is not tolerated, and prejudice of *color* has no existence whatever—the adaptation of that country, by climate, soil and political character, to their physical and political necessities; and the superiority of a residence there over their present position at *home*. It will suffice, that colored men prosecute all the different trades; are store keepers, farmers, clerks and laborers; and are not only unmolested, but sustained and encouraged in any business for which their qualifications and means fit them; and as the resources of the country develop, new fields of enterprise will be opened to them, and consequently new motive to honorable effort.

CHURCHES—SCHOOLS

In the large towns and cities, as in similar communities in other Christian countries, the means for religious instruction are ample.

---

1 *coopers' stuff* Tools for making and repairing casks and barrels.
2 *Dawn* Black agricultural and industrial community founded in 1841, located on the Sydenham river, near the village of Dresden, in present-day southern Ontario.
3 *chattel slavery* Slavery wherein people are regarded as chattel (i.e., as permanently the personal property of an individual owner).

There are costly churches in which all classes and complexions worship, and no "negro pew" or other seat for colored persons especially. I was forcibly struck, when at Toronto, with the contrast the religious community there presented, to our own large body of American Christians. In the churches, originally built by the white Canadians, the presence of colored persons, promiscuously seated, elicited no comment whatever. They are members and visitors, and as such have their pews according to their inclination, near the door, or remote, or central, as best suits them. The number of colored persons, attending the churches with whites, constitutes a minority, I think. They have their "own churches." That that is the feature in their policy, which is productive of mischief to the entire body, is evident enough; and the opinion of the best informed and most influential among them in Toronto and the large towns, is decided and universal. I have heard men of many years residence, and who have, in a measure,[1] been moulded by the better sentiment of society, express deep sorrow at the course of colored persons, in pertinaciously[2] refusing overtures of religious fellowship from the whites; and in the face of all experience to the contrary, erecting Colored Methodist, and Baptist, and other Churches. This opinion obtains amongst many who, when in the United States, were connected with colored churches. Aside from their caste[3] character, their influence on the colored people is fatal. The character of the exclusive church in Canada tends to perpetuate ignorance, both of their true position as British subjects, and of the Christian religion in its purity. It is impossible to observe thoughtfully the working of the incipient Zion, (the Canadian African Church,[4] of whatever denomination,) in its present imperfect state, without seriously regretting that it should have been thought necessary to call it into existence. In her bosom is nurtured the long-standing and rankling prejudices, and hatred against whites, without exception, that had their origin in American oppression, and that should have been left in the country in which they originated—'tis the species of animosity that is not bounded by geographical lines, nor suffers discrimination.

---

1   *in a measure* In part.
2   *pertinaciously* Firmly; unyieldingly.
3   *caste* System of societal division based in class.
4   *the incipient ... Church* I.e., the developing body of an official, exclusively black Church.

A goodly portion of the people in the western part of the Province, (for there are but few in the eastern,) are enjoying superior religious opportunities, but the majority greatly need active missionary effort: first, to teach them love to their neighbor; and, again, to give them an intelligent and correct understanding of the Sacred Scriptures. The missionary strength, at present, consists of but six preachers— active and efficient gentlemen, all of them, and self-sacrificing in the last degree; and several women engaged in teaching, under the same auspices. Much privation suffering, opposition, and sorrow await the missionary in that field. If it were possible for him to foresee what is in store for him there, a mission to India, or the South Sea Islands[1] would be preferable; for, in that case, the sympathy of the entire community is enlisted, and his sojourn is made as pleasant as possible— the people to whom he is sent, are either as little children, simple and confiding, or outright savages; and in that case, deadly enemies. In this less remote field—almost in speaking distance—neglect from friends, suspicion, abuse, misrepresentation, and a degrading surveillance, often of serious and abiding consequences await him. Not directly from the fugitives—those designed primarily to be benefitted—may assaults be looked for, at first. They possess a desire for the light, and incline to cluster around the missionary invariably. There are those who pretend to have been enlightened and to have at heart the common good, whose influence and operations he will find designedly counteracting his conscientious efforts, the more effectively appealing to a common origin and kindred sufferings, secretly striking behind, and bringing his character as a missionary, and his operations, into discredit in the eyes of a sympathizing Christian community. This, and more, awaits those who may be called to the field; but the case is not a hopeless case. The native good sense of the fugitives, backed by proper schools, will eventually develop the real character of their operations and sacrifices. They and their families, of all others, should have the support of Christians.

The refugees express a strong desire for intellectual culture, and persons often begin their education at a time of life when many in other countries think they are too old. There are no separate schools: at Toronto and in many other places, as in the churches, the colored

---

1 *South Sea Islands* Islands in the South Pacific (e.g. Tahiti, Fiji).

people avail themselves of existing schools; but in the western country, in some sections, there is a tendency to "exclusiveness." The colored people of that section petitioned, when the School Law was under revision,[1] that they might have separate schools: there were counter petitions by those opposed, and to satisfy all parties, twelve freeholders among *them* can, by following a prescribed form, demand a school for their children: but if other schools, under patronage of Government exist, (as Catholic or Protestant) they can demand admission into them, if they have not one. They are not compelled to have a colored school. The following is that portion of the school law that directly relates to them:

> And be it enacted, That it shall be the duty of the Municipal Council of any township, and the Board of School Trustees of any city, town, or incorporated village, on the application in writing of twelve or more resident heads of families, to authorize the establishment of one or more separate schools for Protestants, Roman Catholics or colored people and, in such case, it shall prescribe the limits of provisions for the holding of the first meeting for election of Trustees of each separate school or schools as is provided in the fourth section of this Act for holding the first school meeting in a new school section. Provided always that each separate school shall go into operation at the same time with alterations in school sections and shall be under the same regulations in respect to the person for whom such school is permitted to be established, as are common schools generally: Provided, secondly, that none but colored people shall be allowed to vote for the election of Trustees of the separate school for their children, and none but the parties petitioning for the establishment of, or sending children to a separate Protestant or Roman Catholic school, shall vote at the election of Trustees of such schools: Provided thirdly, that each separate Protestant, or Roman Catholic, or colored school, shall be entitled to share in the school fund, according

---

1 *School ... revision* In Upper Canada the Separate School Act of 1850 allowed for any group of five or more black families to petition school trustees for the formation of their own school. Public schools were officially open to all races, but discrimination against black schoolchildren was such that it was often very difficult in practice for them to attend.

to the average attendance of pupils attending each such separate school, (the mean attendance of pupils for both summer and winter being taken,) as compared with the average attendance of pupils attending the common schools in such city, town, village or township: Provided fourthly, that no Protestant separate school shall be allowed in any school division, except when the teacher of the common school is a Roman Catholic, nor shall any Roman Catholic separate school be allowed except when the teacher of the common school is a Protestant.

As before said, the facilities for obtaining a liberal education,[1] are ample in the large towns and cities. In Toronto, students of all complexions associate together, in the better class schools and colleges. The operations of missionaries being chiefly among colored people, they have established several schools in connection with their labors, yet they are open to children without exception. The colored common schools have more of a complexional character than the private, which, with no exception that I have heard of, are open to all. The Act of Parliament above referred to, was designed to afford the fullest and most equable facilities for instruction to all, and that particular clause was inserted with the view to satisfy them, though less objectionable to the body of them, than what they asked for.

The fugitives in some instances, settled on Government land before it came to market, cleared away and improved it. Their friends established schools which were flourishing, when they were obliged to break up, and the people to disperse, because of the inability to purchase and other persons buying. This cause has, in a measure, retarded[2] the spread of general information amongst them.

Again, twenty or more families are often settled near one another, or interspersed among the French, Dutch, Scotch, Irish and Indians, in the woodland districts: often, English is not spoken. There may not be an English school, and all revel together in happy ignorance. Nothing but the sound of the axe, and their own crude ideas of independence to inspire them, unless it be an Indian camp fire occasionally. This may be rather an uninviting state of affairs to those

---

1 *liberal education* Education in a broad range of subjects (as opposed, for example, to technical training).
2 *retarded* Slowed.

living in crowded cities, but it is true there are numerous grown up families, of white and colored, who do not know better. But as uninteresting as is the detail, in this particular aspect of these affairs, the signs are encouraging. If they went to labor honestly, in a region semi-barbarous, they have cut their way out, and are now able to make themselves heard in a demand for religious instructors of the right kind, and schools. Many efficient persons have devoted their time and talents to their instruction, but there has not been anything like an equal number to the work.

Neither are they often found to have materials to work with. Individuals in the United States often send books to those most needy, yet they are usually of such a character as to be utterly useless. I have often thought, if it's really a benevolent act to send old almanacs, old novels, and all manner of obsolete books to them, what good purpose was accomplished, or even what sort of vanity was gratified, by emptying the useless contents of old libraries on destitute fugitives? It would be infinitely better not to give, it seems, though probably persons sending them think differently. The case is aggravated from the fact of a real desire, on the part of the recipients, to learn, and their former want of opportunity. Probably the propensity to give is gratified; but why not give when gifts are *needed* of that which is useful? But the question, if it is answering any good purpose to give such things as books even, has not been satisfactorily answered in the affirmative, to person who have seen the fugitives in their Canadian homes.

SETTLEMENTS—DAWN—ELGIN—THE INSTITUTION—FUGITIVE HOMES

Much has been said of the Canada colored settlements, and fears have been expressed by many that, by encouraging exclusive settlements, the attempt to identify colored men with degraded men of like color in the States would result, and as a consequence, estrangement, suspicion, and distrust would be induced. Such would inevitably be the result, and will be, shall they determine to have entirely proscriptive settlements.[1] Those in existence, so far as I have been

---

1 *proscriptive settlements* I.e., settlements that forbid whites.

able to get at facts, do not exclude whites from their vicinity; but that settlements may not be established of that character, is not so certain. Dawn, on the Sydenham river, [and] Elgin, or King's Settlement,[1] as it is called, situated about ten miles from Chatham, are settlements in which there are regulations in regard to morals, the purchase of lands, etc., bearing only on the colored people: but whites are not excluded because of dislike. When purchase was made of the lands, many white families were residents—at least, locations were not selected in which none resided. At first, a few sold out, fearing that such neighbors might not be agreeable; others, and they the majority, concluded to remain, and the results attest their superior judgment. Instead of an increase of vice, prejudice, improvidence,[2] laziness, or a lack of energy, that many feared would characterize them, the infrequency of violations of law among so many is unprecedented; due attention to moral and intellectual culture has been given; the former prejudices on the part of the whites, has given place to a perfect reciprocity of religions and social intercommunication. Schools are patronized equally; the gospel is common, and hospitality is shared alike by all. The school for the settlers at Elgin, is so far superior to the one established for white children that the latter was discontinued, and, as before said, all send together, and visit in common the Presbyterian church, there established. So of Dawn; that settlement is exceedingly flourishing and the moral influence it exerts is good, though, owing to some recent arrangements, regulations designed to further promote its importance are being made. Land has increased in value in those settlements. Property that was worth but little, from the superior culture given by colored person over the method before practiced and the increasing desires for country homes, is held much higher. Another fact that is worth a passing notice is that a spirit of competition is active in their vicinity. Efforts are now put forth to produce more to the acre, and to have the land and tenements[3] present a tidy appearance. That others than those designed to be benefitted by the organization, should be, is not reasonable, else might persons, not members of society justly

---

1 *Dawn ... Settlement* Both Elgin and Dawn were black communal experiments. In Upper Canada (from 1841 to 1867, Canada West; thereafter, Southern Ontario), all such settlements were located in the southwestern part of the province.

2 *improvidence* Lack of foresight; thoughtlessness.

3 *tenements* Buildings.

claim equal benefits with members. If Irishmen should subscribe to certain regulations on purchasing land, no neighboring landholders could rightfully share with them in the result of the organization. But prejudice would not be the cause of exclusion. So it is of those two settlements: it cannot be said of them, that they are caste institutions, so long as they do not express hostility to the whites; but the question of their necessity in the premises may be raised, and often is, by the settlers in Canada as well as in the States. The "Institution" is a settlement under the direction of the A.M.E. Church;[1] it contains, at present, two hundred acres, and is sold out in ten acre farms, at one dollar and fifty cents per acre, or one shilling less than cost. They have recently opened a school, and there is a log meeting house in an unfinished state, also a burying ground. There are about fifteen families settled on the land, most of whom have cleared away a few trees, but it is not in a very prosperous condition, owing, it is said, to bad management of agents—a result to be looked for when a want of knowledge characterize them. This "Institution" bids fair to be one nucleus around which caste settlements will cluster in Canada.

The Refugees' Home[2] is the last settlement of which I may speak in this place. How many others are in contemplating I do not know, though I heard of a least two others. This Society is designed to appropriate fifty thousand pieces of land for fugitives from slavery, only, but at present the agents have in possession two hundred acres, situated about eight miles from Windsor, in the western district. The plan is to sell farms of twenty-five acres, that is, to give five acres to actual settlers, with the privilege of buying the adjoining twenty acres at the market value—one third of the purchase money constitutes a fund for school and other purposes; and ten years are given to pay for the twenty acres but no interest may accumulate. This society may now

---

1 *A.M.E. Church* African Methodist Episcopal Church, founded in 1816 by Richard Allen (1760–1831). Shadd had long been a member while living in the United States, but broke with the church after moving to Canada over the issue of its growing tendency towards "exclusiveness" (segregation).

2 *The Refugees' Home* Shadd broke with Henry Bibb, co-founder of the Refugees Home, on matters of principle (notably, his support for exclusivity of blacks from whites, and his desire to extend assistance only to former slaves and not to those who had suffered as "free" citizens). But (as Rosemary Sadlier details in her biography of Shadd), she also took issue with Bibb's handling of financial affairs—specifically, that he was a "dishonest man" who had diverted funds to his own purposes that should have gone to assist others.

be considered in operation as they have made a purchase, though, as yet, no one has settled thereon, and the results to be looked for from it, from the extent of the field of operations, will have an important hearing on the colored people who are now settled in Canada, or who may emigrate thither. The friends of the society, actuated by benevolent feelings towards victims of American oppression and the odious Fugitive Law, are sanguine as to the success of the measure, but not so universal is the opinion in its favor, even among those designed to be benefitted; in fact, all the objections raised against previously existing settlement, hold good against these, with the additional ones of greater magnitude. It is well known that the Fugitive Bill makes insecure every northern colored man—those free are alike at the risk of being sent south. Consequently many person, always free, will leave the United States and settle in Canada, and other countries, who would have remained had not that law been enacted. In pro-slavery communities, or where colonization influence prevails, they would leave at a sacrifice; they arrive in Canada destitute, in consequence, but may not settle on the land of the Refugees' Home, from the accident of nominal freedom, when it is well known that even slaves south, from the disgrace attending manual labor when performed by whites, have opportunities, in a pecuniary way, the colored men have not in some sections north. Again, the policy of slaveholders, has been to create a contempt for free people in the bosom of their slaves, and pretty effectually have they succeeded. Their journey to Canada for liberty has not rooted out prejudice, quite, and reference to man's birth as free or slave, is generally made by colored persons, should he not be as prosperous as his better helped fugitive brethren. Thus, discord among members of the same family, is engendered; a breach made, that the exclusive use by fugitives of the society lands is not likely to mend. Again the society, with its funds, is looked upon in the light of a powerful rival standing in the way of poor free men, with its ready cash, for its lands will not all be government purchases; neither does it contemplate large blocks, exclusively, but, as in the first purchase, land, wherever found, and in small parcels also. From the exclusive nature of the many settlements, (as fugitive homes,) when it shall be known for what use it is wanted, individual holders will not sell but for more than the real value, thus embarrassing poor men who would have bought on time, and as an able purchaser from government, the society must have a first choice. The objections in common with other settlements, are: the individual supervision of resident agents, and the premium indirectly offered for good behavior. "We are free men," say they who advocate independent effort, "we, as other subjects, are amenable to British laws; we wish to observe and appropriate to ourselves, whatever of good there is in the society around us, and by our individual efforts, to attain to a respectable position, as do the many foreigners who land on the Canada shores, as poor in purse as we were; and we do not want agents to beg for us." The accompanying are articles in the Constitution:

Article 2.   The object of this society shall be to obtain permanent homes for the refugees in Canada, and to promote their moral, social, physical, intellectual, and political elevation.

Article 11.   This society shall not deed lands to any but actual settlers, who are refugees from southern slavery, and who are the owners of no land.

Article 12.   All lands purchased by this society, shall be divided into twenty-five acre lots, or as near as possible, and at least one-tenth of the purchase price of which shall be paid down by actual settlers before possession is given, and the balances to be paid in equal annual instalments.

Article 13.   One-third of all money paid in for land by settlers, shall be used for education purposes, for the benefit of said settlers' children, and the other two-thirds for the purchase of more lands for the same object, while chattel slavery exists in the United States.

By-Laws

Article 1.   No person shall receive more than five acres of land from the society, at less than cost.

Article 4.   No person shall be allowed to remove any timber from said land until they have first made payment thereon.

These are the articles of most importance, and, as will be seen, they contemplate more than fifty thousand acres of continual purchases, till slavery shall cease; and other terms, as will be seen by Article 13 of Constitution, and Article 4, By-Laws, that most fugitives just from slavery can comply with, (as destitute women with families, old men, and single women,) until after partial familiarity with their adopted, country. This, say many colored Canadians, begins not to benefit until a man has proven his ability to act without aid, and is fit for political equality by his own industry, that money will get for him at any time.

POLITICAL RIGHTS—ELECTION LAW—OATH—CURRENCY

There is no legal discrimination whatever effecting colored emigrants in Canada, nor from any cause whatever are their privileges sought to be abridged. On taking proper measures, the most ample redress can be obtained. The following "abstracts of acts," bearing equally on all, and observed fully by colored men qualified, will give an idea of the measure given them;

> The qualifications of voters at municipal elections in townships, are freeholders and householders of the township or ward, entered on the roll for rateable real property, in their own right or that of their wives, as proprietors or tenants, and resident at the time in the township or ward.
>
> In towns, freeholders and householders for rateable real property in their own names or that of their wives, as proprietors or tenants to the amount of £5 per annum or upwards, resident at the time in the ward. The property qualification of town voters may consist partly of freehold and partly of leasehold.[1]

In villages it is £3 and upwards, with freehold or leasehold; in cities £8.

---

1 *The qualifications ... leasehold* As Richard Almonte has noted, this and the other long quotations in this chapter are from *Scobie's Canadian Almanac* for 1852.

The laws of regulating elections, and relation to electors, are not similar in the two Canadas;[1] but colored persons are not affected by them more than others:

> No person shall be entitled to vote at county elections, who has not vested in him, by legal title, real property in said country of the clear value of forty-four shillings and five pence and one farthing, currency. Title to be fee simple or freehold under tenure of free and common soccage, or in fief in roture, or in franc allen, or derived from the Governor and Council of the late Province of Quebec, or Act of Parliament. Qualificatiori, to be effective, requires actual and uninterrupted possession on the part of the elector, or that he should have been in receipt of the rents and profits of said property for his own use and benefit at least six months before the date of the writ of election. But the title will be good without such anterior possession, if the property shall have come by inheritance, devise, marriage or contract of marriage, and also if the deed or patent from the Crown on which he holds to claim such estate in Upper Canada have been registered three calendar months before the date of the writ of election. In Lower Canada, possession of the property under a written promise of sale registered, if not a notarial deed, for twelve months before the election, to be sufficient title to vote. In Upper Canada, a conveyance to wife after marriage must have been registered three calendar months, or husband have been in possession of property six months before election.
>
> Only British subjects of the full age of twenty-one are allowed to vote. Electors may remove objection by producing certificate, or by taking the oath.

These contain no proscriptive provisions, and there are none. Colored men comply with these provisions and vote in the administration of affairs. There is no difference made whatever; and even in the slight matter of taking the census it is impossible to get at the exact number of whites or colored, as they are not designated as such. There is, it is

---

1   *the two Canadas* Upper Canada and Lower Canada (the present Southern Ontario and Southern Quebec).

true, petty jealousy manifested at times by individuals, which is made use of by designing; but impartiality and strict justice characterise proceedings at law, and the bearing of the laws. The oath, as prescribed by law is as follows:

"I, A.B., do sincerely promise and swear, that I will bear faithful and true allegiance to Her Majesty Queen Victoria, as lawful Sovereign of the United Kingdom of Great Britain and Ireland, and of this Province of Canada, dependents on and belong to the said United Kingdom, and that I will defend her to the uttermost of my power against all traitors, conspiracies and attempts whatever which shall be made against Her Person, Crown and Dignity, and that I will do my utmost endeavor to disclose and make known to Her Majesty, Her Heirs and Successors all treason and traitorous conspiracies and attempts which I shall know to be against Her or any of them, and all this I do swear without any equivocation, mental evasion, or secret reservation, and, renouncing all pardons and dispensations from person whatever, to the contrary. So help me God."

The Deputy Returning Officer may administer oath of allegiance to persons who, according to provisions of any Act of Parliament, shall become, on taking such oath, entitled to the privileges of British birth in the Province.

Persons knowing themselves not be qualified, voting at elections, incur penalty of £10; and on action brought, the burden of proof shall be on the defendant. Such votes null and void.

The qualifications of Municipal Councillors are as follows:— Township Councillors must be a freeholder or householder of the township or ward ... as proprietor or tenant rated on the roll, in case of a freeholder for £100 or upwards; householder for £200 or upwards: Village Councillor, in case of a freeholder for £10 or upwards; a householder for £20 and upwards: Town Councillor, in case of a freeholder £20 per annum; if a householder to the amount of £40 and upwards. The property qualification of Town Councillors may be partly freehold and partly leasehold.

A tenant voter in town or city must have occupied by actual residence, as a separate tenant, a dwelling house or houses for twelve months of the yearly value of £11 2s. 1½d. currency, and have paid a year's rent, or that amount of money for the twelve months immediately preceding the date of election writ. A person holding only a shop or place of business but not actually residing therein, is not entitled to vote. And a voter having changed his residence within the town during the year, does not affect his right to vote, but must vote in the ward in which he resides on that day.

Articles Exempt from Duty

The following are some of the articles exempt from duty on importation:

"Models of machinery and other inventions and improvements in the arts. Horses and carriages of travelers; and horses, cattle and carriages and other vehicles when employed in carrying merchandize together with the necessary harness and tackle, so long as the same shall be *bona fide* in use for that purpose, except the horses, cattle, carriages and harness of persons hawking goods, wares and merchandize through the Province for the purpose of retailing the same, and the horses, cattle, carriages and harness of any circus or equestrian troop for exhibition; the horses, cattle, carriages and harness of any to be free,"

Donations of clothing specially imported for the use of or to be distributed gratuitously by any charitable society in the Province.

Seeds of all kinds, farming utensil and implement of husbandry, when specially imported in good faith by any society incorporated or established for the encouragement of agriculture.

Wearing apparel in actual use, and other personal effects not merchandize; horses and cattle; implements and tools of trade of handicraftsmen.

… Trees, shrubs, bulbs and roots; wheat and Indian corn; animals, specially imported for the improvement of stock; paintings, drawings, maps, busts, printed books, (not foreign reprints of British copy-right works,) ashes, pot and peal, and soda.

CURRENCY OF CANADA

Gold		Currency		
The British Sovereign when of full weight		£1	4s	4d.
U.S. Eagle, coined before 1st July 1834		£1	13s	4d.
U.S. Eagle, between 1st July 1834, and 1st July 1851		£2	10s	0d.

Silver			Silver		
British Crown	6s	1d.	Other eight silver dollar	0s	6d.
Half Crown	3	0	U.S. sixteenth dollar	0	3½
Shilling	1	2	Other sixteenth dollar	0	3
Sixpence	0	7½	Five franc piece	4	8
The dollar	5	1			
Half dollar	2	6½	Copper		
U.S. quarter dollar	1	3	British penny	0	1
Other eighth dollar	1	0	British half penny	0	0½
U.S. eighth dollar	0	7½	British farthing	0	0¼

ABSTRACT OF LAW OF SUCCESSION IN UPPER CANADA[1]

*** Be it therefore enacted, &c., That whenever, on or after the first day of January, which will be in the year of our Lord one thousand eight hundred and fifty-two, any person shall die [seized?] in fee simple or for life of another of any real estate in Upper Canada, without having lawfully devised the same, such real estate shall descend or pass by way of succession manner following, that is to say:

Firstly—To his lineal descendants, and those claiming by or under them, *per stirpes*.[2]

---

1 [Shadd's note] (14 and 15 Vic. Cap. 6—185) Scobie. [Shadd in this instance provides the exact reference to *Scobie's Almanac of 1852*.]

2 *per stirpes* Latin: by roots. This is a legal term used in discussions of inheritance; if an estate is divided among the children of the deceased *per stirpes*, each child inherits an equal portion. (If one child were already deceased, that portion would pass to the child's own children, etc.)

Secondly—To his father

Thirdly—To his mother: and

Fourthly—To his collateral relatives.[1]

Subject in all cases to the rules and regulation hereinafter prescribed.

2. That if the intestate[2] shall leave several descendants in the direct line of lineal descent, and all of equal degree of consanguinity[3] to such intestate, the inheritance shall descend to such person in equal parts, however remote from the intestate the common degree of consanguinity may be.

3. That if any of the children of such intestate be living, and any be dead, the inheritance shall descend to the children who are living, and to the descendants of such children as shall have died, so that each child who shall be living shall inherit such share as would have descended to him if all the children of the intestate who shall have died, leaving issue, had been living, and so that the descendants of each child who shall be dead shall inherit the share which their parents would have received, if living, in equal shares....

18. The children and relatives who are illegitimate shall not be entitled to inherit under any of the provisions of this Act.

THE THIRTY THOUSAND COLORED FREEMEN OF CANADA

The colored subjects of her Majesty in the Canadas are, in the general, in good circumstances, that is, there are few cases of positive destitution to be found among those permanently settled. They are settled promiscuously in cities, towns, villages, and the farming districts; and no equal number of colored men in the States, north or south, can produce more freeholders. They are settled on, and own portions of the best farming lands in the province, and own much valuable property in the several cities, etc. There is, of course, a difference in the relative prosperity and deportment in different sections, but a respect for, and observance of the laws, is conceded

---

1 *collateral relatives* Persons of shared ancestry, but not of direct lineage.

2 *the intestate* Those who die without leaving a will.

3 *consanguinity* Level of blood relation; shared ancestry.

to them by all; indeed, much indifference on the part of the whites has given place to genuine sympathy, and the active abolitionists and liberal men of the country, look upon that element in their character as affording ground for hope of a bright future for them, and as evidence that their sympathy for the free man is not misplaced, as more than compensation for their own exertions for those yet in bonds. I have said, there is but little actual poverty among them. They are engaged in the different trades and other manual occupations. They have a paper conducted by the Rev. Henry Bibb,[1] and other able men, white and colored, are laboring among them, and in view of the protection afforded, there is no good reason why they should not prosper. After the passage of the fugitive law, the sudden emigration of several thousand in a few months, destitute as they necessarily were, from having, in many instances, to leave behind them all they possessed, made not a little suffering for a brief period, (only among them,) and the report of *their* condition had an injurious bearing upon all the colored settlers. Clothing, provisions, and other articles were sent them, but often so disposed of, or appropriated, as not to benefit those for whom intended. Distrust of agents, indiscriminately, and altogether but little real good has followed from the charity. The sensible men among them, seeing the bad results from a general character for poverty and degradation, have not been slow to express their disapprobation[2] in the social circle, in meetings, and through the public papers. The following extracts express fully the sentiments of nine-tenths of the colored men of Canada; they think they are fully able to live without begging. There are others (very ignorant people,) who think differently, as there will be in all communities, though they are in the minority, there are those, also, and they are a respectable minority, (in point of numbers,) who are in favor of distinctive churches and schools, and of being entirely to themselves; they will come in for especial notice, but first, let us hear the people of Buxton[3] and other places:

---

1   *paper ... Bibb*   Bibb's *Voice of the Fugitive*, founded in 1851, was the first black newspaper publication in Canada.

2   *disapprobation*   Strong moral disapproval.

3   *Buxton*   Center of the Elgin black settlement.

If facts would bear out the statements made, the fugitives would have little to choose between slavery on one side of the line, and starvation on the other; but we rejoice that he is not reduced to the alternative. The man who is willing to work need not suffer, and unless a man supports himself he will neither be independent nor respectable in any country.... The cry that has been often raised, that we could not support ourselves, is a foul slander, got up by our enemies, and circulated both on this and the other side of the line, to our prejudice. Having lived many years in Canada, we hesitate not to say that all who are able and willing to work can make a good living.... It is time the truth should be known concerning the relief that has been sent to the "suffering fugitives in Canada," and to what extent it has been applied. The boxes of clothing and barrels of provisions which have been sent in, from time to time, by the praiseworthy, but misguided zeal of friends in the United States, has been employed to support the idle, who are too lazy to work, and who form but a small portion of the colored population in Canada. There are upwards of thirty thousand colored persons in Canada West, and not more than three thousand of them have ever received aid, and not more than half of them required it had they been willing to work. We do not think it right that twenty-seven thousand colored persons, who are supporting themselves by their own industry, should lie under the disgraces of being called public beggars, when they receive nothing, and don't want anything.... We wish the people of the United States to know that there is one portion of Canada West, where the colored people are self-supporting, and they wish them to send neither petticoat nor pantaloons to the county of Kent.... The few cases of real want which arise from sickness or old age, can, with a trifling effort, be relieved here, without making it a pretext for a system of wholesale begging in the United States.

EDWARDS R. GRANTS
SAMUEL WICKHAM   Committee.[1]
ROBERT HARRIS

---

1 *Committee* The letter was published in *Voice of the Fugitive* on 8 April 1852, with the names of the committee that Shadd lists. Very little is known about the three men listed as members of the committee.

As to the state of things in Toronto and in Hamilton, I can say, from actual observation, that extreme suffering is scarcely known among the black people, while some who are far from being as industrious and deserving as they ought to be, receive aid to which they would hardly seem entitled.—*S.R. Ward's letter to the Voice of the Fugitive.*[1]

Notwithstanding the prosperity and liberal sentiment of the majority, there is yet a great deal of ignorance, bigotry, prejudice, and idleness. There are some who are only interested in education so far as the establishment of separate schools, churches, &c., tend to make broad the line of separation they wish to make between them and the whites; and they are active to increase their numbers, and to perpetuate, in the minds of the newly arrived emigrant or refugee, prejudices, originating in slavery, and as strong and objectionable in their manifestations as those entertained by whites towards them. Every casual remark by whites is tortured into a decided and effective negro hate. The expressions of an individual are made to infer the existence of prejudice on the part of the whites, and partiality by the administrators of public affairs. The recently arrived fugitives, unacquainted with the true state of things, is *completely convinced* by the noisy philippic[2] against all the "white folks," and all colored ones who think differently from them, and he is thus prepared to aid demagogues[3] in preventing the adoption of proper measure for the spread of education and general intelligence, to maintain an ascendency over the inferior minds around them, to make the way of the missionary a path of thorns. Among that portion, generally, may those be found, who by their indolent habits, tend to give point to what of prejudice is lingering in the minds of the whites; and it is to be feared that

---

1   *S.R. Ward's ... Fugitive* Samuel Ringgold Ward (1817–66), who had been born into slavery, escaped with his family while still a child, and lived in New Jersey and New York State until 1851, when he emigrated to Canada. He became active in the Anti-Slavery Society of Canada, and published a series of letters in *Voice of the Fugitive* in 1851 to 52. His reputation was such that when Shadd founded her own newspaper, the *Provincial Freeman*, she initially used Ward's name on the masthead, listing him as editor even though it was in reality almost entirely her enterprise. (The fiction was abandoned in 1854.)

2   *philippic* Bitter attack or denunciation.

3   *demagogues* Political leaders who seek support by appealing to popular prejudices.

they may take some misguided step now, the consequences of which will entail evil on the many who will hereafter settle in Canada. The only ground of hope is in the native good sense of those who are not making use of the same instrumentalities for[1] improvement as are the whites around them.

THE FRENCH AND FOREIGN POPULATION

The population of Canada consists of English, Scotch, French, Irish and Americans; and, including colored persons, numbers about 1,582,000. Of the whites, the French are in the majority, but the increasing emigration of Irish, Scotch, English and other Europeans, is fast bringing about an equality in point of numbers that will be felt in political circles. In Canada West the French are in the minority.

The disposition of the people generally towards colored emigrants, this is, so far as the opinions of old settlers may be taken, and my own observation may be allowed, is as friendly as could be looked for under the circumstances. The Yankees, in the country and in the States adjoining, leave no opportunity unimproved to embitter their minds against them. The result is, in some sections, a contemptible sort of prejudice, which, among English, is powerless beyond the individual entertaining it—not even affecting *his circle*. This grows out of the constitution of English society, in which people are not obliged to think as others do. There is more independent thought and free expression than among Americans. The affinity between the Yankees and French is strong; said to grow out of similar intentions with respect to political affairs: and they express most hostility, but it is not of a complexional character only, as that serves as a mark to identify men of a different policy. Leaving out Yankees—having but little practical experience of colored people—they, (the French,) are pre-disposed, from the influence alluded to, to deal roughly with them; but in the main benevolence and a sense of justice are elements in their character. They are not averse to truth. There is a prevailing hostility to chattel slavery, and an honest representation of the colored

---

1 *instrumentalities for* Means of.

people: their aims and progressive character, backed by uniform good conduct on their part, would in a very short time destroy every vestige of prejudice in the Province.

> The public mind literally thirsts for the truth, and honest listeners, and anxious inquirers will travel many miles, crowd our country chapels, and remain for hours eagerly and patiently seeking the light.... Let the ignorance not prevalent on the subject of slavery be met by fair and full discussion, and open and thorough investigation, and the apathy and prejudice now existing will soon disappear.—*S.R. Ward.*

Colored persons have been refused entertainment in taverns, (invariably of an inferior class,) and on some boats distinction is made: but in all cases, it is that kind of distinction that is made between poor foreigners and other passengers, on the cars and steamboats of the Northern States. There are the emigrant train and the forward deck in the United States. In Canada, colored persons, holding the same relation to the Canadians, are in some cases treated similarly. It is an easy matter to make out a case of prejudice in any country. We naturally look for it, and the conduct of many is calculated to cause unpleasant treatment, and to make it difficult for well-mannered person to get comfortable accommodations. There is a medium between servility and presumption, that recommends itself to all person of common sense, of whatever ranks or complexion: and if colored people would avoid the two extremes, there would be but few cases of prejudices to complain of in Canada. In cases in which tavern keepers and other public characters persist in refusing to entertain them, they can, in common with the traveling public generally, get redress at law.

Persons emigrating to Canada, need not hope to find the general state of society as it is in the States. There is as in the old country, a strong class feeling—lines are as completely drawn between the different classes, and aristocracy in the Canadas is the same in its manifestations as aristocracy in England, Scotland and elsewhere. There is no approach to Southern chivalry, nor the sensitive democracy prevalent at the North; but there is an aristocracy of birth, not of skin, as with Americans. In the ordinary arrangements of society, from wealthy and titled immigrants and visitors from the mother country, down through the intermediate circles to Yankees and Indians, it appears to have been settled by common consent, that one class should not "see any trouble over another"; but the common ground on which all honest and respectable men meet, is that of innate hatred of American slavery.

RECAPITULATION

The conclusion arrived at in respect to Canada, by an impartial person, is, that no settled country in America offers stronger inducements to colored people. The climate is healthy, and they enjoy as good health as other settlers, or as the native; the soil is of the first quality; the laws of the country give to them, at first, the same protection and privileges as to other person not born subjects; and after compliance with Acts of Parliament affecting them, as taking oath, &c., they may enjoy full "privileges of British birth in the Province." The general tone of society is healthy; vice is discountenanced,[1] and infractions of the law promptly punished; and, added to this, there is an increasing anti-slavery sentiment, and a progressive system of religion.

THE BRITISH WEST INDIES—MEXICO—SOUTH AMERICA—AFRICA

Inducements have been held out by planters to colored men, to settle in the British West Indies, and agents have been sent particularly from Jamaica and Trinidad, from time to time, to confer with them on the subject. The prominent feature in their efforts, has been the direct advantage to the planter from such emigration. The advantages to be derived by settlers, in a pecuniary point, from any system of emigration originating with proprietors of estates, will be doubtful so long as the present mode of planting, managing and involving estates, continues, if the emigrants consent to be mere laborers instead of owners of the soil. But from a system of voluntary emigration to those islands, different results may be looked for. The former method would

---

1   *discountenanced* Not approved of.

but degrade them, the latter materially elevate them. The vicinity of those islands to the southern United States makes it necessary that they should be peopled by colored men and *under British protection*; in short, that they should be British subjects. The policy of the dominant party in the United States, is to drive *free* colored people out of the country, and to send them to Africa, only, and at the same time, to give the fullest guaranty to slaveholders, for the continuance of their system. To fulfil, to the letter, this latter, they make large calculations of a future interest in the West Indies, Honduras, and ultimately South America. They wish to consecrate to slaver and the slave power the portion of this continent; at the same time they deprecate the vicinity of freemen. To preserve those countries from the ravages of slavery, should be the motive to their settlement by colored men. Jamaica, with its fine climate and rich soil, is the key to the gulf of Mexico. It is not distant from the United States, Cuba, nor Haiti; but, as if providentially,[1] is just so positioned that, if properly garrisoned by colored free men, may, under Britain, promptly and effectually check foreign interference in its own policy, and any mischievous designs now in contemplation toward Cuba and Haiti. So of that portion of the isthmus now under the protection of Great Britain.[2] In view of the ultimate destiny of the southern portion of North America, it is of the first importance that colored men strengthen that and similar positons in that region. They are the natural protectors of the Isthmus and the contiguous country: it is said by medical men, that those of the human family, physically capable of resisting the influences of great heat, are also capable of enduring severe cold; and the varied experiences of colored person in America, proves that they live to as great age as whites, whether as whalemen in the northern seas, and settlers in the British provinces, (far north of the United States,) or in the West Indies. The question of availability, can never be raised, for this time there are those who conduct with great ability the business of the Islands.[3] Colored men are greatly in the majority, not more than one-sixth are whites. They are legislators, lawyers, physicians, ministers, planters, editors, merchants, and laborers;

---

1   *providentially* Opportunely; as if ordained by divine foresight.
2   *that portion ... Britain* The colony of British Honduras, founded in 1862, which became the nation of Belize in 1981.
3   *Islands* Caribbean Islands; the West Indies.

and they demonstrate clearly their capacity for self-government, and the various departments of civil life, by the great change in their condition since emancipation. The story of loss from the emancipation act,[1] is a gross misrepresentation, gotten up by interested parties for the benefit of slavery. True there may not be so much exported as formerly, for the very good reason that there are more purchasers at home. The miserably fed slave of former days, is now the independent *free* man, with the ability to buy whatever his judgment prompts him to. Neither is the demand for laborers for large estate evidence that the peasantry are idle. There are more small farmers and cultivators on their own account, more store-keepers and traders, and they of the emancipated class. More attention is, of course, paid to education, and the children are thus relieved, in a measure, from outdoor duties. Much has been done by the colored people of those islands to improve their condition, and much more may be done conjointly with emigrants from the States, to perfect society, strengthen the British in that quarter, and thus keep up the "balance of power." It needs no prophet to foretell the establishment of an empire formed out of the southern United States and Mexico. The settlement by colored people of those countries, with their many sympathizers, is but a preparatory step: that step has been taken, slavery and republican rapacity will do the rest. Under what more favorable auspices could emigration to the West Indies be made than the present, now that a general welcome would be extended by the people to those who would like a milder climate than the States? What government is so powerful and so thoroughly impartial, as Her Majesty's; so practically anti-slavery, and so protective? None. The objection that we wish our own government to demonstrate our capacity for self-government is done away with at once, for there are colonies controlled, so far as their immediate affairs extend, by colored men. The assertion that white men universally degrade colored, is disproved by the facts. There is no "aristocracy of skin"; every incentive to honorable effort is kept before them. It is of the first importance, then, that the government of those islands should be anti-slavery, and that only governments, anti-slavery in sprit and tendency, and having a liberal religious policy, should be sought

---

1 *story ... act* Some conservative commentators claimed that the Abolition of Slavery Act in 1833 had resulted in economic loss. Canada West was one of the British colonies affected by this emancipation act.

out by colored people from the United States. They, of all others on this continent have drank plentifully of the cup of degradation, made more bitter from the never ending parade about freedom. They would be powerful auxiliaries of the present inhabitants, in forming a will of defense, or available for offensive operations, as a *decided protest,* for instance, as the best interests and policy of the British government might demand.

Those who oppose emigration from the United States, say, "you (colored people,) will not desire to be the laborers in other countries; to dig the canals, work on rail roads, ditch, and the like, but you will prefer to engage in trade, and that others will forestall you." Men who are honest in their desire for a change, who love liberty better than slavery, or who are unwilling to await the tedious process by which, in the United States, their rights will be given, if ever, will not be fastidious on emigrating to a country. Emigrants to any country, who should aim at a monopoly of the so called respectable occupations, exclusively, would be looked upon with distrust, as well as contempt, and the result to the emigrant would not be far different from a monopoly of menial employments. There will be no scarcity of land, and a medium, between the extensive operations of capitalists, and the degrading occupations of colored people, generally, in the crowded cities of the United States, thus opens to them a certain road to future eminence, in every way preferable to the sudden changes and chances of trade, exclusively.

Allusion is at times made to South America, and plans for a grant of territory from governments in that country, in which to form an "independent government," have been proposed. Others say, "unite with existing governments." Neither plan can recommend itself to prospective emigrants generally. In the first place, there is no precedent on record of a grant, similar to the one sought, and the policy of independent governments, with respect to each other, would always be opposed to unqualified grants. The great objection to uniting with those governments at present, would be their want of toleration in matters of religion; so long as the intimate connexion of the State with the Romish Church[1] exists, those countries must be but a poor asylum for the oppressed. The liberals, with them, form a minority,

---

1   *Romish Church* I.e., the Catholic Church.

struggling for life against the exaction of popery, and the ambition of military chiefs. Would colored men be prepared to adopt the religion of the country? That with them would be the only guaranty of protection, such "protection as vultures give to lambs."[1] "Let us seize upon Africa, or some other, unappropriated territory while we may," say others, "and establish our own governments." But Africa has already been seized upon; the English, French, Portuguese, Spanish and Turks, have long since shared her out among themselves, and little Liberia may yet revert to some heir-at-law, who has purposely been unmindful of her. There is yet Mexico, to be spoken of hereafter, and a southern continent, but that belongs to the United States, it may be by right of discovery; so there seems to be no safe alternative left but to be satisfied with the government now existing that is most reliable and most powerful. The government is Great Britain; her dependencies form a *secure* home for the American slave, and the disgraced *free* man. The last of her possessions to which I shall call attention in this place, is Vancouver's Island.

MEXICO

The vicinity of Mexico to the United States, and the known hostility of Mexicans to the institution of slavery, weigh strongly with some person in favor of emigration to that country; but on careful consideration, it will be seen that that country does not present the features, in the main, that the States of South America do. The hankering of the old Castilians after lost power, is much greater in Mexico than farther south; and to regain that there would not be scruples about a coalition with American Slaveholders, even. The spirit of democracy has never so thoroughly pervaded that country, and those under the shadow of Simon Bolivar.[2] Mexico was called New Spain. In her was remodeled the prominent features of Spanish policy in Europe. There was the grand center point of Spanish dignity,

---

1 *protection ... lambs* From Act 2, Scene 2 of Richard Brinsley Sheridan's play *Pizarro* (1799), about the conquest of Peru.
2 *shadow ... Bolivar* Simón Bolívar (1783–1830) was an early Venezuelan President and influential leader in the Latin American Wars of Independence. His "shadow" thus affected the independent nations of Bolivia, Columbia, Ecuador, Peru, and Venezuela.

religious intolerance, and regal domination, for the New World. In the States of South America, a change of policy was a necessity growing out of the relations of the Church of Rome to society generally. In Mexico; it was an earnest demand of the majority to throw off the Spanish yoke. This is shown in the relative position of the Church in those countries. In Mexico the Roman Catholic Church is in undisputed supremacy, and the Pope is to them the ultimatum. In the states of South America, though that religion prevails, yet concession has been made, by Rome, in the person of a dignitary of equal powers there with the Pope elsewhere. With them the Pope is but little more respected than the Greek Patriarch. In those States, except Peru, (in which there is but one idea generally among Natives and Spanish,) there was no previously civilized class, continually brooding over Spanish wrong: the natives came to terms, and they and Creoles combined to destroy Spanish tyranny backed by Rome, consequently, after victory over Spain was achieved by them, their remaining enemy was and is the Church in its modified form. It yet has, as before said, sufficient influence to make these countries undesirable for colored people from the United States in the present phase of things.

We want a strong position. Mexico does not offer that, even though the majority are anti-slavery. The Southern United States have "marked her for their prey," which she will be for a time; and combining with the minority, the probability is a contest for the supremacy of slavery for a long time. If it were certain that slavery would not be tolerated but for a short period, still the move would be inexpedient,[1] as direct contact with revolutionary movements, or other plans of progress, in her present state affecting it, would be inevitable. The position of colored Americans must be a conservative one, for a time, in any foreign country (from the very nature of their relations to foreign nations), as well as for themselves in the United States; and it were folly in them to voluntarily enter the breach between any two hostile nations until stronger in position. Their efforts, to be rational, should be to gain strength. People who love liberty do not emigrate to weak governments to embroil themselves in their quarrels with stronger ones, but to strong ones, to add to their strength and better their own condition, and foreigners fighting for others, are, generally, either

---

1 *inexpedient* Impractical; unadvisable.

hirelings, or isolated adventurers striving after fame. Whatever people go to Mexico and adopt her institutions, must calculate beforehand, to set aside the habits of independent civil life—must for a long time, repudiate the plough, the arts, and trade, with their concomitants, in a great country or make them but secondary in importance to the, there, paramount ideas of military life, and the certainty of frequent attacks from abroad and at home. The weakness, or rather the internal feuds of Mexico, invite attack from unscrupulous parties, is it meet[1] then that emigrants of any nation should make haste to "settle there"? We look in vain for the precedent of emigration to a country distracted even to bloodshed, with internal feuds, by any people; and we may look in vain for prosperity. In advocating this, we would leave out of sight, the check that a fortifying of the West Indies with our emigrants would give to depredations on the contiguous countries, and only gratify the love to fight, without immediate advantage.

Let Mexico, at present, take care of herself, by the efforts of her own mixed population rightly directed, and let our emigrants so *abolitionize*[2] and strengthen neighboring positons as to promote the prosperity and harmony of the whole. This can be done without compromising away honor; in fact the sentiment "liberty or death," is never realized but by so proceeding as to secure the first permanently, and only courting the latter when life is no longer of utility. I know that the recollection of innumerable wrongs, makes the desire for payment in like coin the necessity of some men's natures, but no real end is attained after all: the Indians have learned sense from frequent defeat, the consequence of going to war before they were prepared, and whole tribes now cultivate the arts of peace and progress. Let us learn even of savages! We can get up a fight at any time, but who is the wiser for the sight? No one, honest men would but try to suppress it, so would a coalition with any nation, and especially a weak one, to carry out retaliatory measures, result.

The pro-slavery party of the United States is the aggressive party on this continent. It is the serpent that aims to swallow all others. It is meet then to make strongholds, and, if need be, defend them; that will be the most effective check to greediness of land and negroes.

---

1 *meet* Suitable or proper.
2 *abolitionize* Convert people into abolitionists.

This island is situated between 49° and 51° north latitude, or on the southern boundary of British America; and between 122° and 127° west longitude. It is about three hundred miles long, and between ninety and one hundred miles broad, and contains about twenty-eight thousand square miles. Though remotely situated and comparatively uninhabited, (there being not more than twenty thousand persons on it,) it will, it is said, be the first island in importance on the globe. It has a fine climate, being in the same latitude as the south of England, Germany, and the north of France: the soil is also of the best description. But it is not as an agricultural island that it will surpass all others. The Western Continent, and particularly the northern part, say "wise men of the east," must eventually leave the eastern far in the distance, (a fact that should not be lost sight of by colored men,) and that over the Pacific will the trade with eastern nations be prosecuted.[1] It is important now as a stopping place for whale ships visiting the Northern Seas, and is directly in the route to the East Indies, Japan Isles, and China, from Oregon and British America. The overland route to Pacific terminating near the point, the great Atlantic trade of Western Europe and America will find there the most practicable outlet and the shortest distance to Eastern Asia; consequently the people there settled, of whatever complexion, will be the "merchant princes of the world," and under the protection of Great Britain. Now, there are two weighty reasons why the people settled there should be colored principally; the first, because by that means they would become more fully involved in the destiny of this Continent; any eastern move of magnitude, as for instance to Africa, if *possible,* would appear a retrograde step, now that the current of affairs is so clearly setting west: and secondly, in no more effectual-way could a check be given to the encroachments of slavery on free soil. The purely American sympathy for "kith and kin" only, would experience unmistakable obstacles to its free exercise, in the event of a contemplated annexation of that delightful Western country.

It will be seen, that the possibility of a pretty extensive emigration to those countries has been the prominent feature throughout this

---

1 *prosecuted* Executed; conducted.

tract, and for that reason direct reference has been made to other points under British jurisdiction, than Canada. The preference given to these, (Canada, West Indies, and Vancouver's Island,) over British Colonies elsewhere, has been because of their strong position and availability in every way. There would not be as in Africa, Mexico, or South America, hostile tribes to annoy the settler, or destroy at will towns and villages with their inhabitants: the strong arm of British power would summarily punish depredations made, of whatever character, and the emigrants would naturally assume the responsibility of British freeman.

The question whether or not an extensive emigration by the free colored people of the United States would affect the institution of slavery, would then be answered. I have here taken the affirmative of that question, because that view of the case seems to me most clear. The free colored people have steadily discountenanced any rational scheme of emigration, in the hope that by remaining in the States, a powerful miracle for the overthrow of slavery would be wrought. What are the facts. More territory has been given up to slavery, the Fugitive Law has passed, and a concert of measure, seriously affecting their personal liberty, has been entered into by several of the Free states; so subtle, unseen and effective have been their movements, that, were it not that we remember there is a Great Britain, we would be overwhelmed, powerless, from the force of such successive shocks; and the end may not be yet, if we persist in remaining for targets, while they are strengthening themselves in the Northwest, and in the Gulf. There would be more of the right spirit, and infinitely more of real manliness, in a peaceful but decided demand for freedom to the slave from the Gulf of Mexico, than in a miserable scampering from state to state, in a vain endeavor to gather the crumbs of freedom that a pro-slavery besom[1] may sweep away at any moment. May a selection for the best be made, now that there are countries between which and the United States a comparison may be instituted. A little folding of the hand, and there may be no retreat from the clutches of the slave power.

—1852

---

1 *besom* Broom made of twigs.

Provincial Freeman.

DEVOTED TO ANTI-SLAVERY, TEMPERANCE, AND GENERAL LITERATURE.

VOLUME I.]   TORONTO, CANADA WEST, SATURDAY, NOVEMBER 18, 1854.   [NUMBER 36.

Front page of the 18 November 1854 issue of the *Provincial Freeman*, the newspaper that Shadd founded and edited for several years in the 1850s.

In Context

1. from Harriet Martineau, *Society in America* (1838)

Harriet Martineau's two-volume account of her extended travels in the United States is an invaluable source on a great many topics of relevance to Shadd's *Plea for Emigration*. It provides description and commentary on the institution of slavery itself; on the network of laws erected to protect that institution (including the widespread censorship of anti-slavery materials in the South, the criminalization of manumission by slave owners who wished to free any of their slaves, and the criminalization of efforts by others to assist slaves to freedom); on the severe persecution endured by nominally free black citizens in northern states; and on "charitable" efforts by whites to support the "re-colonization" of blacks in Africa. As such, it provides helpful background concerning the circumstances of fugitive slaves seeking to escape to Canada, as well as those of the free "people of color" whom Shadd believed should also have the opportunity to emigrate.

from VOLUME 1, CHAPTER 3, SECTION VI ("CITIZENSHIP OF PEOPLE OF COLOR")

Before I entered New England, while I was ascending the Mississippi, I was told by Boston gentlemen that the people of color in the New England states were perfectly well treated; that the children were educated in schools provided for them; and that their fathers freely exercised the franchise. This gentleman certainly believed he was telling me the truth. That he, a busy citizen of Boston, should know no better, is as striking ... as a correct representation of the facts would have been.... [He] was not aware that the schools for the colored children in New England are, unless they escape by their insignificance, shut up, or pulled down, or the school house wheeled away upon rollers over the frontier of a pious state, which will not endure that its colored citizens should be educated. He was not aware of a gentleman of color, and his family, being locked out of their own hired pew in a church, because their white brethren will not worship by their side....

A Connecticut judge lately a footnote recently declared on the bench that he believed people of color were not considered citizens in the laws. He was proved to be wrong. He was actually ignorant of the wording of the acts by which people are termed citizens. ...

They are citizens. They stand as such in the law, and in the acknowledgment of everyone who knows the law. They are citizens, yet their houses and schools are pulled down and they can obtain no remedy at law. They are thrust out of offices, and excluded from the most honourable employments, and stripped of all the best benefits of society by fellow citizens who, once a year, solemnly lay their hands on their hearts, and declare that all men are born free and equal, and that rulers derive their just powers from the consent of the government.

from VOLUME 2, CHAPTER 1, "AGRICULTURE," SECTION II ("RURAL LABOR")

Of the many [slave owning] families [which I met], there was, I believe, none where I was not told of some one slave of unusual value, or talent for goodness, either in a present or a former generation. A collection of these [testimonies] alone, as they stand in my journal, would form new mean (slight) testimony to the intellectual and moral capabilities of Negros. ... [T]he consideration which binds me to silence upon a rich collection of facts, full of moral beauty and promise, is regard [for] the safety of many whose heroic obedience to the laws of God has brought them into jeopardy under the laws of slave holders, and the allies of slave holders.[1]

Nor would I, by any careless revelations, throw the slightest obstacle in the way of the escape of any one of the slaves who may be about to shirk[2] their masters, by methods with which I happen to be acquainted.

It can, however, do nothing but good to proclaim the truth that slaves do run away in much greater numbers than is supposed by any

---

1   *the laws of ... slave holders* Elsewhere in her work Martineau says, while defending abolitionists, that "their only political transgression [and who will call it a moral one?] is helping fugitive slaves." (See Volume 2, "Morals of Slavery.")

2   *shirk* Run away from.

but those who lose them, and those who help them…. [E]verybody who has been in America is familiar with the little newspaper picture of a black man, hieing with his stick and bundle, which is prefixed to the advertisements of runaways. Every traveller has probably been struck with the number of these which meet his eye; but unless he has more private means of information, he will remain unaware of the streams of fugitives continually passing out of the States. There is much reserve about this in the South, from pride; and among those elsewhere who could tell, from far other considerations. The time will come when the whole story, in its wonder and beauty, may be told by some who, like myself, have seen more of the matter, from all sides, than it is easy for a native to do. Suffice [to say] that the loss by runaways, and the general useless attempts to recover them, is a heavy item in the accounts in the cotton and sugar growers of the south; and one which is sure to become heavier till there should be no more bondage to escape from. It is obvious that the slaves who run away are among the best—an escape being usually the achievement of a project early formed, concealed, pertinaciously adhered to, and endeared by much toil and sacrifice undergone for its sake for a long course of years…. Of the cases known to me, the greater number of the men, and some of the women, have acted throughout upon an idea (called by their owners "a fancy"—a very different thing), while some few of the men have started off upon some sudden infliction of cruelty; and many women on account of intolerable outrage of the grossest kind….

It is proposed by the Colonization Society that free persons of color shall be sent to establish and conduct a civilized community on the shores of Africa. The variety of prospects held out by this proposition to persons of different views is remarkable. To the imaginative, there is the picture of the restoration of the colored race to their paternal soil: to the religious, the prospect of evangelizing Africa. Those who would serve God and mammon [at the same time] are delighted at being able to work their slaves during their own time, and then leave them to the Colonization Society with a bequest of money, (when money must needs be left behind), to carry them over to Africa. Those who would be doing, in a small way, immediately, let certain of their slaves work for wages which are to carry them over to Africa. Those who have slaves too clever or discontented to be safe neighbours, can ship them off to Africa. Those who are afraid of the rising intelligence of their free colored neighbours, or suffer strongly under the prejudice of color, can exercise such social tyranny as shall drive such troublesome persons to Africa. The clergy, public lecturers, members of legislatures, religious societies, and charitable individuals, both in the north and south, are believed to be, and believe themselves to be, labouring on behalf of slaves, when they preach, lecture, obtain appropriations, and subscribe, on behalf of the Colonization Society. Minds and hearts are laid to rest—opiated into a false sleep.

Here are all manner of people associated for one object, which has the primary advantage of being ostensibly benevolent ... it has the aid, for twenty years, of almost all the presses and pulpits of the United States, and of most of their politicians, members of government, and leading professional men and merchants, and almost all the planters of 12 states, and all the missionary interest. Besides the subscriptions arising from so many sources, there have been large appropriations made by various legislatures. What is the result?—nothing. "*Ex nihilo nihil fit*"[1]....

In twenty years, the Colonization Society has removed to Africa between two and three thousand persons; while the annual increase of the slave population, by the lowest computation, is sixty thousand; and the number of free blacks is upwards of three hundred and sixty two thousand....

As far as I could learn, no leading member of the Colonization Society has freed any of his slaves. Its president had sold twelve, the week before I first saw him.... and so it is, through the whole hierarchy. ... it appears to me that the Colonization Society could never have gained any ground at all, but for the common supposition that the blacks must go somewhere. It was a long while before I could make anything of this. The argument always ran thus: "Unless they remain as they are, Africa is the only place for them. It will not do to give them a territory; we have seen enough of that with the Indians. We are heartsick of territories. The Blacks would all perish. Then, the climate of Canada would not suit them: they would perish there. The Haitians would not take them in: they have a horror of freed slaves. There is no rest for the soles of their feet, anywhere in Africa!"

---

1   *Ex nihilo nihil fit*   Latin: Out of nothing nothing will be made.

"Why should they not stay where they are?"

"Impossible. The laws of the States forbid freed Negros to remain."

"At present—on account of the slaves who remain. In case of abolition such laws would be repealed, of course. And then, why should not the blacks remain where they are?"

"They could never live among the Whites in a state of freedom."

"Why? You are begging the question."

"They would die of vice and misery."

"Why more than [for example] the German labourers?"

"They do in the free States. They are dying out there constantly."

"What makes them more vicious than other people?"

"The colored people always are."

"You mean because their color is the badge of slavery?"

"Yes."

"Then, when it is no longer so, the degradation, for aught you know shall cease."

This is the circle described by those who pity the slaves. There is another, apropos to ... the masters.

"What is to become of the planters, without any labourers? They must shut up and go away; for they cannot stay in their houses, without any labourers on the plantations."

"Are the slaves to be all buried? or are they to evaporate? or what?"

"Oh, you know, they would all go away. Nothing would make them stay when they were once free."

"They would change masters, no doubt. But as many would remain in the area as before. Why not?"

"The masters could not possibly employ them. They could never manage them, except as slaves."

"So you think that the masters could not have the labourers, because they would go away: and the labourers must go away, because the masters would not have them."

To prevent any escape ... in this circle, the other is brought up rounded, to prove that there is no other place than Africa for the blacks to go to: and thus, the alternative of slavery or colonization is supposed to be established.

All conversation on ... this institution bears the same character— of arguing in a circle.

There are, as is well known throughout the country, houses in the free states which are open to fugitive slaves, and where they are concealed till the search for them is over. I know some of these secrets of such places; and can mention two cases, among many, of runaways, which shows how horrible is the tyranny which the slave system authorizes men to inflict on each other. A Negro had found his way to one of these friendly houses; and had been so skillfully concealed, that repeated searches by his master, (who had followed for the purpose of recovering him), and by constables, had been in vain. After three weeks of this seclusion, the Negro became weary, and entreated of his host to be permitted to look out of the window. His host strongly advised him to keep quiet, as it was pretty certain that his master had not given him up. When the host had left him, however, the Negro came out of his hiding place, and went to the window. He met the eye of his master, who was looking up from the street. The poor slave was obliged to return to his bondage.

A young Negress had escaped in like-manner; was in like-manner concealed; and was alarmed by constables, under the direction of her master, entering the house in pursuit of her, when she had had reason to believe that the search was over she flew upstairs to her chamber in the third story, and drove a heavy article of furniture against the door. The constables pushed in, not withstanding, and the girl leapt from the window into the paved street. Her master looked at her as she lay, declared she would never be good for anything again and went back into the south. The poor creature, her body bruised, and her limbs fractured, was taken up, and kindly nursed; and she is now maintained in Boston, in her maimed condition, by the charity of some ladies there.

2. from Frederick Douglass, *Life of an American Slave* (1845)

Douglass, an escaped slave who became the leading African American figure of the nineteenth century, was a powerful advocate for the abolition of slavery—and, later in the century, against the ongoing persecution of African Americans by the white majority. Douglass spoke out strongly against segregation in all its forms—very much including the various schemes put forward to "repatriate" black people to Liberia or other parts of Africa, or to encourage emigration to the Caribbean or Latin America. (Such plans were promoted by societies founded by blacks as well as societies founded by whites.) Douglass was unequivocal: "the native land of the American Negro is America." Indeed, he held to this view so strongly that, as the passage below indicates, he felt that efforts to assist African Americans to emigrate to Canada for their own safety were also misguided.

Similarly, after the Civil War, Douglass opposed the movement of African Americans north from the southern states to escape the oppression of Jim Crow legislation. In the 1880s and 1890s, however, he altered his views, disillusioned with America's continuing failure to address the ills of racial oppression.

from Chapter 11

I now come to that part of my life during which I planned, and finally succeeded in making, my escape from slavery. But before narrating any of the peculiar circumstances, I deem it proper to make known my intention not to state all the facts connected with the transaction. My reasons for pursuing this course may be understood from the following: First, were I to give a minute statement of all the facts, it is not only possible, but quite probable, that others would thereby be involved in the most embarrassing difficulties. Secondly, such a statement would most undoubtedly induce greater vigilance on the part of slaveholders than has existed heretofore among them; which would, of course, be the means of guarding a door whereby some dear brother bondman might escape his galling chains. I deeply regret the necessity that impels me to suppress any thing of importance connected with my experience in slavery. It would afford me great pleasure indeed, as well as materially add to the interest of my narrative, were I at liberty to gratify a curiosity, which I know exists in the minds of many, by an accurate statement of all the facts pertaining to my most fortunate escape. But I must deprive myself of this pleasure, and the curious of the gratification which such a statement would afford. I would allow myself to suffer under the greatest imputations which evil-minded men might suggest, rather than exculpate myself, and thereby run the hazard of closing the slightest avenue by which a brother slave might clear himself of the chains and fetters of slavery.

I have never approved of the very public manner in which some of our western friends have conducted what they call the *underground railroad*, but which I think, by their open declarations, has been made most emphatically the *upperground railroad*. I honor those good men and women for their noble daring, and applaud them for willingly subjecting themselves to bloody persecution, by openly avowing their participation in the escape of slaves. I, however, can see very little good resulting from such a course, either to themselves or the slaves escaping; while, upon the other hand, I see and feel assured that those open declarations are a positive evil to the slaves remaining, who are seeking to escape. They do nothing towards enlightening the slave, whilst they do much towards enlightening the master. They stimulate him to greater watchfulness, and enhance his power to capture his slave. We owe something to the slave south of the line as well as to those north of it; and in aiding the latter on their way to freedom, we should be careful to do nothing which would be likely to hinder the former from escaping from slavery. I would keep the merciless slaveholder profoundly ignorant of the means of flight adopted by the slave. I would leave him to imagine himself surrounded by myriads of invisible tormentors, ever ready to snatch from his infernal grasp his trembling prey. Let him be left to feel his way in the dark; let darkness commensurate with his crime hover over him; and let him feel that at every step he takes, in pursuit of the flying bondman, he is running the frightful risk of having his hot brains dashed out by an invisible agency. Let us render the tyrant no aid; let us not hold the light by which he can trace the footprints of our flying brother. But enough of this. I will now proceed to the statement of those facts, connected with my escape, for which I am alone responsible, and for which no one can be made to suffer but myself.

3. from William H. Smith, *Smith's Canadian Gazetteer* (1846)

Smith states in his preface that he was "induced to undertake the task" of writing his gazetteer by the "great ignorance" which he found to exist respecting the province of Canada West (now Ontario), "not only amongst the persons in Great Britain, or newly arrived emigrants, but even amongst many of those who had been for years resident in the country." The *Gazetteer* included information on all towns and geographical areas in the province. The following excerpts are taken from the section of general reflections with which the work concludes.

It is most extraordinary, so long as Canada has been settled, that its great natural advantages should still be so little known; that so many persons who are either compelled by necessity to emigrate, or who do so from choice, should continue to pass it by and go on to the west of the United States, or otherwise emigrate to the more distant colonies of the Cape, New South Wales, or New Zealand and yet such is the case....

In what respects will the advocates of emigration to the United States pretend to say that any portion of that country is superior to Canada. Is it the climate? A tree may be judged of by its fruits, and very many of the native Canadians, in point of robust appearance and complexion, might be taken for English emigrants. Will any one venture to make the same assertion respective a native of Ohio, Indiana, Illinois, or Missouri? And of what avail is it that the climate will grow cotton and tobacco, if the settler neither has the strength to cultivate them, nor a market in which to dispose of them, when grown? In the winter and spring of 1841–42, pork (a staple article of the State) was selling in Illinois, at from a dollar to a dollar and a half per 100 lbs.; and at that price it was almost impossible to obtain cash for it; wheat at a quarter dollar, and Indian corn from five to ten cents per bushel; butter, fifteen and sixteen pounds for a dollar; fowls, half a dollar per dozen; and other farming produce in proportion. At such prices farming could not be very profitable. A man certainly might live cheaply, and cram himself with bacon and corn bread till he brought on bilious fever;[1] but he could *make nothing* of what he raised. And a farmer having a fat ox, has even been known after killing it, to take from it the hide and tallow, and drag the carcass into the woods to be devoured by the wolves; finding from the small price

---

1   *bilious fever* Over-secretion of bile, causing indigestion.

the beef would fetch, that it was more profitable to do so than to sell the whole animal!

Is it from the nature of the government, that the States are so much more desirable as a place of residence—where the only law is mob law, and the bowie knife is the constant companion of the citizens, and is used even in the halls of legislature themselves? Or is New Zealand much to be preferred, where the settler in taking his morning ramble, to acquire an appetite for his breakfast, frequently receives a "settler" himself, and instead of returning to his morning's meal, is roasted for the breakfast of some native chief, and his interesting family. Canada, on the contrary, suffers under none of these disadvantages and annoyances. The government and constitution of the country are English; the laws English; the climate is fine and healthy; the Indians are tolerably civilized, none of them at any rate are cannibals, and few of them are even thieves; and bowie knives are not "the fashion." The settler, unless he has been guilty of the folly of planting himself down beyond the bounds of civilization and of roads, may always command a fair price and cash for whatever he can raise—he need never be beyond the reach of medical attendance, churches, and schools—he can obtain as much land as he need wish to purchase, at a fair and moderate rate—he knows that whatever property he acquires is as secure as if he had it in England—his landed property, if he possesses any, is gradually increasing in value—and if he is only moderately careful and industrious, he need have no anxiety for the future—his sons, growing up in and with the country, and as they grow, acquiring a knowledge of the country and its customs, and the various modes of doing business in it, if steady, will have no difficulty in succeeding in any business they may select, or may be qualified for.

Much has been written on the subject of emigration, and many speculations entered into as to *who* are the proper persons to emigrate? The only answer that can be given to this question is—*those who are obliged to do so*. Let no person who is doing *well* at home, no matter what may be his profession or occupation, emigrate with the expectation of doing *better*—let him not leave his home and travel over the world, in search of advantages which he may not find elsewhere. But those who are *not* doing well, who find it difficult to struggle against increasing competition, who fear the loss in business of what little property they possess, or who find it difficult with an increasing family to keep up appearances as they have been accustomed to do, and find it necessary to make change—all these may safely emigrate, with a fair prospect of improving their condition. Persons of small, independent incomes may live cheaply in Canada, particularly in the country, and enjoy many comforts, and even luxuries, that were not within their reach at home. Retired military men do not generally make good settlers. They usually, when they leave the army, sell out, instead of retiring on half pay; and when they emigrate they are apt to squander their property in purchasing land and in building, till at length they come to a stand for want of the means to proceed, frequently with their buildings half-finished, from being planned on too large a scale; although, if they had been asked in the commencement how they intended to live when the ready money was expended, they would have been unable to give an intelligible answer. If they succeed in getting some government office, the emoluments[1] of which are sufficient for their support, they will manage to get along very well; otherwise they will sink gradually lower and lower, and their children are apt to get into idle and dissipated habits. The idle and inactive life to which they have been accustomed while in the army, particularly during these "piping times of peace,"[2] totally incapacitates them for making good settlers in the backwoods. *A lounger, unless independent, has no business in Canada.* Naval officers, on the contrary, make settlers of a very different character. They have been accustomed, when on service, to a life of activity; and if they have been long on service, they have generally seen a great deal of the world—they have their half-pay to fall back on, which fortunately for them they cannot sell—and they generally make very excellent settlers. Lawyers are not wanted: Canada swarms with them; and they multiply in the province so fast, that the demand is not by any means equal to the supply. Medical men may find many openings in the country, where they will have no difficulty in making a tolerable living; but they will have to work hard for it, having frequently to ride fifteen, twenty-five, or even thirty miles to see a patient! And in the towns, the competition is as great as in England....

---

1 *emoluments* Salary, remuneration.
2 *piping ... peace* See William Shakespeare's *Richard III* 1.1.24: "Why, I, in this weak piping time of peace, / Have no delight to pass away the time."

4. from The Fugitive Slave Act (1850)

Section 6. And be it further enacted, that when a person held to service or labor in any State or Territory of the United States, has heretofore [escaped] or shall hereafter escape into another State or Territory of the United States, the person or persons to whom such service or labor may be due, or his, her, or their agent or attorney ... may pursue and reclaim such fugitive person, either by procuring a warrant from some one of the courts, judges, or commissioners aforesaid, ... or by seizing and arresting such fugitive, where the same can be done without process, and by taking, or causing such person to be taken, forthwith before such court, judge, or commissioner, whose duty it shall be to hear and determine the case of such claimant in a summary manner.... and upon satisfactory proof being made, ... to use such reasonable force and restraint as may be necessary, under the circumstances of the case, to take and remove such fugitive person back to the State or Territory whence he or she may have escaped.... In no trial or hearing under this act shall the testimony of such alleged fugitive be admitted in evidence; and the certificates in this and the first section mentioned, shall be conclusive of the right of the person or persons in whose favor granted, to remove such fugitive to the State or Territory from which he escaped, and shall prevent all molestation of such person or persons by any process issued by any court, judge, magistrate, or other person whomsoever.

Section 7. And be it further enacted, That any person who shall knowingly and willingly obstruct, hinder, or prevent such claimant, his agent or attorney, or any person or persons lawfully assisting him, her, or them, from arresting such a fugitive from service or labor, either with or without process as aforesaid, or shall rescue, or attempt to rescue, such fugitive from service or labor, from the custody of such claimant, ... or shall aid, abet, or assist such person so owing service or labor as aforesaid, directly or indirectly, to escape from such claimant ...; or shall harbor or conceal such fugitive, so as to prevent the discovery and arrest of such person, ... shall, for either of said offences, be subject to a fine not exceeding one thousand dollars, and imprisonment not exceeding six months, ... and shall moreover forfeit and pay, by way of civil damages to the party injured by such illegal conduct, the sum of one thousand dollars for each fugitive so lost as aforesaid....

5. from the *Provincial Freeman*, 24 March 1854

The three pieces included here all appeared in the 24 March 1854 issue of the paper. The first two are unsigned editorials, in all likelihood written by Shadd herself. The third was reprinted in the *Provincial Freeman* from the *Toronto Globe* and includes the editorial preface to the address that had appeared in that paper.

RELATIONS OF CANADA TO AMERICAN SLAVERY

The fact that this is a British Province, and that slavery has no existence on British soil, the fact that this soil never was polluted by slaver, and the fact that (since the ever memorable Somerset decision[1]) the slave of another country became a freeman by touching our soil, place us in relations of antagonism to slavery. This was early seen and felt by the slave, and as early seen and felt by the slaveholder. Accordingly, so early as 1825, the attention of the U.S. Government was directed to this point. In the month of May, of that year, the House of Representatives passed a resolution calling upon the President to enter into correspondence with the British Government, for the recovery of slaves who had escaped into Canada.... From that time to 1842, the number of slaves escaping to Canada constantly and rapidly increased. Then, when a treaty was made between the two Governments, called the Ashburton Treaty, it was most earnestly sought, on the part of the United States Government ... to have an article inserted which should authorize slave catching in Canada; ... but the Court of St. James[2] promptly refused ... to allow the American slaveholder to use Canada as a park to chase human game in.... Canada, therefore, from her connection with the British Crown, is legally and constitutionally in an attitude of antagonism to American slavery. She offers and secures to the American slave, the moment he arrives here, Freedom—British Freedom—impartial Freedom. And when he has stood his seven years' probation, and taken the oath of

---

1 *Somerset decision* Landmark 1772 legal ruling that was popularly interpreted to mean that slavery was illegal in Britain, though not in its colonies—and that a slave automatically became free upon entering Britain.
2 *Court of St. James* Court of the British sovereign, concerned primarily with foreign affairs.

allegiance, Canada secures to him, at home and abroad, in law and in equity, all the rights and immunities of a British subject.

But there is another view of our relations to this subject. It is painful to admit it ... but disgraceful as it is, it is useless to conceal it. Friendliness to slavery is to be found in this Province in more forms than one.

1. There are some parties here who practised slave-driving in the South. They love slavery as they love the gain they derived from wielding the whip over its victims. A sprinkling of such customers is to be found here and there, the Province over.

2. There are others, too, who have married heiresses to slave estates. Having received their wives and slaves by the same act of matrimony, they are strongly tempted to regard slavery to be as sacred as marriage itself.

3. Then there are persons resident in Canada who were once slaveholders in the West Indies. The glorious people of Great Britain, determined to have the great principle of British freedom applied practically to the enslaved, as well as to all others, like Job, they, through the Government, "broke the jaws of the wicked, and delivered the spoiled out of their teeth."[1] But these ex-slaveholders were never convinced of the sin of slave-holding—or, if convinced of it, they then were converted from it. Hence they are in spirit now, what they were in practice before the act of '32.[2] The influence of these parties is as deeply and wickedly pro-slavery as that of the vilest slaveocrats of New York, Boston, Philadelphia or Baltimore.

4. As a born Yankee, we are ashamed of it, but it is true that too many of the natives of the United States have brought their pro-slaveryism with them, from the other side. Like the refugee slaves, they come here to enjoy an improvement of their condition, and like them, too, they enjoy the protecting care of

---

1   *broke the ... their teeth* Cf. Job 29.17.
2   *act of '32* The Act for the Abolition of Slavery throughout the British Colonies was in fact passed by Parliament in August 1833, and began to take effect in August 1834.

this good British realm; but they turn scornfully upon the black man, and do what [they can] to rob him of his rights—to which the latter is as fully entitled as themselves. From sympathy with their native country, and from their own negro-hate, they maintain a constant and growing pro-slavery influence wherever they are settled. There are but very few exceptions to this rule, for it is a rule; and most safely may it be said, that while the Yankees are far from being the only negro-haters, or pro-slavery parties, whose principles disgrace our country, it is nevertheless true that the mass of them are the most decided slaveocrats in the land; and what is more, they most industriously spread and promulgate their sentiments, and seek to make them prevalent and controlling, even to the violation of Her Majesty's laws. We could give abundant illustrations of this.

5. It remains to be said, that the prejudice against negroes, so prevalent in various parts of the Province, as maintained by many persons of all nations, including, of course, native Canadians, is one of the strongest pro-slavery influences that disgraces and degrades our fair county; it does more to place us side by side with American oppressors than any other thing. Everybody knows that it is the North and not the South that supplies the power of public opinion, of the pulpit, the press, commerce, manufactures, literature, religion, politics, everything that keeps slavery alive. Now the sentiment—the controlling sentiment of the people of the North, that renders them the volunteer bodyguard of slavery—is their negro-hate. The maintenance of a like negro-hate here, of course, encourages the same feeling there, and aids it in doing its very worst work. Every Canadian negro-hater is a volunteer British slaveocrat. Every such one is a strengthener of the slave system, and we repeat, that there should be such, is one of the worst facts—the foulest disgrace, the deepest degradation—in all our history.

So long as these facts exist, we shall want anti-slavery labors, organizations, agitation, and newspapers in Canada. Our humble life shall be devoted to the counteracting of the pro-slaveryism of our adopted country. It is for this reason that we leave our own hearthstone, and expose ourselves to so many disagreeables, as a lecturing agent of the Canadian Anti-Slavery Society. Hence it is we consent, without pay, to scribble for the Provincial Freeman. And we do believe that the education and improvement of our own people will lay this enmity to liberty and humanity—this friendship for despotism—low, in a death and burial that shall know no resurrection, and that at no very distant day. At any rate we shall labor on in hope.

Let the pro-slaveryism of Canada be overcome, and let the anti-slavery influence of our laws, constitution, and position be fully and freely exerted, and there is no portion of the British Empire whose influence against slavery would be so healthful and so potent as that of Canada.

Union

We have frequently heard it said that no people are so much given to party divisions, dissensions and disunions as the colored people. But we question the correctness of this very prevalent opinion. The Irish are divided into Orangemen[1] and Catholics; the Scotch into Highlanders and Lowlanders; the English into as many divisors as there are counties in England almost. Then each of these dislikes, and is divided against all the rest. Come to religious denominations, and any town in the British Empire will furnish abundant proof that the black people are very far from either enjoying or suffering a monopoly of disunionism. The truth is, that in this respect, the colored people are precisely like any other people, especially are they like any other ignorant people;[2] and the more we see of other people, the more deeply are we impressed, not only with the oneness, but with the likeness of the human family, in this, as in all other respects.

Some fear that the differences of opinion existing among our people, in respect to certain public matters, will prove disastrous. We have no such fears. It would be no mark of manliness in us, to think, according to the dictum of every man assuming

---

1 *Orangemen* I.e., Prostestants.
2 *ignorant people* I.e., people who are denied the benefits of education.

to be a leader among us, or who should please to lord it over us. We freely confess that we desire no union at the expense of free independent thinking and action. We ask no one blindly to follow, or agree with us, upon the pain of being denounced as a disunionist; and He who made us knows, that we will follow no demagogue, black or white, in doctrine or practice, into that which our judgment and conscience disapprove, for fear of incurring the blame of any who esteem union as of all things most valuable. Union is desirable—very desirable—and worthy of forbearance, forgiveness, self-denial, and charity for its obtainment; but union purchased at the expense of moral principle, is purchased at too dear a rate.[1] It is better to stand alone, upon principle, than to go with any multitude, compromising principle.

American Slavery

[The following address to the Women of the Union States has been prepared by the Toronto Ladies Association for the relief of Destitute Colored Fugitives. It is written in a good spirit, and contains suggestions which it is the legitimate province of women to carry out into practical action. Much may be effected by female influence, especially in family arrangements, and in the education of those who are to be the future legislators and the wives of legislators. There is about this address also what will commend it the more to the people of the United States—a plainness of speech which they like. It expresses the truth in courteous terms, and seeks not to sweeten the unpalatable fact that slavery is a sin which ought to be abolished at once by every Christian nation—Globe.]

The affectionate address of thousands of the women of Canada to their sisters, the women of the United States of America.

"While the women of England, with whom we in this Colony are identified, propose to address you on the subject of Negro

---

1   *at too dear a rate* Too expensively.

Slavery, it may not seem an unfitting occasion for us to add, in the name of Christian spirit, our suggestions and entreaties. Living so near to the scene of slavery, and coming daily into contest with its bitter fruits, in the persons of those unhappy fugitives who have been compelled by law to seek an asylum in our country, we cannot but deeply deplore its continuance in the world, and especially in your mighty nation—a nation whose influence for good might be co-extensive with the civilized world, were it not for this foul blot, which mars its glory and paralyzes its power.

"We would then ask you, in the spirit of Christian love, to use that influence which, as sisters, as daughters, and as mothers, you possess, for the abolition of a system, which deprives its victims of the fruits of their labor; which substitutes concubinage for the sacred institution of marriage; which abrogates the relation of parent and child, tearing children from the arms of their parents, and parents from each other; which shrouds the intellect of rational beings in the dark gloom of ignorance and forbids the souls of immortal beings from holding communion with their maker; and which degrades man, created in the Divine image, to the level of a beast. We repeat not this dark catalogue of crimes, needlessly to wound your feelings, or in a spirit of self complacency, as if we and our fathers were free from all guilt, but with the view of sufferers. We ask you to ponder seriously and dispassionately the fact that the system which generates such evils is becoming daily more deeply rooted in your soil, and hence more difficult to be cured or eradicated. We presume not to dictate to you the mode of action to which your sympathies should lead, but would affectionately suggest the following as peculiarly suited to your sex: to soften the harsh and cruel, to remonstrate with the unfeeling and unjust, to confirm the wavering and to encourage the timid. We do not forget that there are many masters of slaves, who like Patrick Henry, confess their guilt, and so far pay 'their devoirs to virtue as to own the excellence and rectitude of her precepts, and lament their want of conformity to them.'[1] In the case of such, use your influence to win them into the path of virtue. We believe that there are many who, like your celebrated Pinckney, declare 'that by the eternal principles of natural justice, no master in the State has a right to hold his slave in bondage a single hour' but who are yet timid in their action.[2] Encourage and determine such by your counsel and approbation. In the quiet seclusion of domestic privacy, warn those who desire to extend the area of slavery, of the difficulties that surround its present limits, and beseech them to think of the final results. Above all, let mothers prayerfully imbue the youthful hearts of their children with those important scripture truths which declare 'That God hath made out of one blood all nations of men to dwell on all the face of the earth.'[3] 'There is no respect of persons with God.'[4] 'Forbear threatening, for both your and their master is in heaven.'[5] 'Give unto your servants (slaves) that which is just and equal.'[6] 'Do unto others as you would that they should do unto you;'[7] and we venture

---

1   *like Patrick Henry ... conformity to them* The American founding father Patrick Henry (1736–99) twice served as Governor of Virginia. Famous for his rousing oratory against the British in the period leading up to the American Revolution ("Give me liberty or give me death," he famously declared), Henry never did grant liberty to his own slaves. The passage quoted here is from a 13 January 1773 letter to John Alsop, a Quaker who had written to Henry to plead the case against slavery. Henry declared that he would "honor the Quakers for their noble efforts to abolish Slavery," and acknowledged that he remained an owner of slaves merely from "the general inconvenience of living without them." Nevertheless, he remained a slave owner and defender of slavery in the circumstances of his own time. The furthest he would go in that context was to urge that slaves be treated leniently:

> I will not—I cannot justify [slavery], however culpable my conduct. I will so far pay my devoir to Virtue, as to own the excellence and rectitude of her precepts, and to lament my want of conformity to them. I believe a time will come when an opportunity will be afforded to abolish this lamentable evil. Everything we can do, is to improve it, if it happens in our day; if not, let us transmit to our descendants, together with our slaves, a pity for their unhappy lot, and an abhorrence of slavery. If we cannot reduce this wished-for reformation to practice, let us treat the unhappy victims with lenity. It is the furthest advancement we can make toward justice.

2   *Pinckney ... action* Charles Cotesworth Pinckney (1746–1825), a South Carolina politician who ran twice for the presidency. Though he owned slaves and defended the institution of slavery, he had supported the abolition of the slave trade in 1808.
3   *That God ... the earth* Cf. Acts 17.26.
4   *There is ... with God* Cf. Romans 2.11.
5   *Forbear ... heaven* Cf. Ephesians 6.9.
6   *Give unto ... and equal* Cf. Colossians 4.1.
7   *Do unto ... unto you* Cf. Matthew 7.12.

to predict that ere another generation pass away 'every bond shall be broken,'[1] and the oppressed will go free; and your great Republic, free from its heavy incubus, will then truly be a land in which 'all men are equal, and have a right to life, liberty, and the pursuit of happiness.' Women of America, your power for good is great, and great are your responsibilities. Many of you by your talents, your advocacy of the rights and liberties of mankind, and your self-denying labors on behalf of the injured African race, command the admiration of mankind. To encourage such in their works of love, and to arouse others to use more energetically the means with which Nature hath endowed them for similar purposes, we now venture to address you, and earnestly pray that to you, the women of the United States, may belong the imperishable honor of removing from your soil the iniquitous system of slavery, which that noble spirit—the ornament of your country—Judge Jay,[2] has described as 'a sin of crimson dye,' and the 'abolition of which in your land was amongst the first wishes of the immortal Washington.'"

---

1   *every bond shall be broken* Phrase commonly used in anti-slavery rhetoric. Also cf. Isaiah 58.6.
2   *Judge Jay* John Jay (1745–1829). One of the founding fathers of the United States, Jay was a leading opponent of slavery. In 1789 he became the first Chief Justice of the United States.

From the Publisher

A name never says it all, but the word "Broadview" expresses a good deal of the philosophy behind our company. We are open to a broad range of academic approaches and political viewpoints. We pay attention to the broad impact book publishing and book printing has in the wider world; we began using recycled stock more than a decade ago, and for some years now we have used 100% recycled paper for most titles. Our publishing program is internationally oriented and broad-ranging. Our individual titles often appeal to a broad readership too; many are of interest as much to general readers as to academics and students.

Founded in 1985, Broadview remains a fully independent company owned by its shareholders—not an imprint or subsidiary of a larger multinational.

For the most accurate information on our books (including information on pricing, editions, and formats) please visit our website at www.broadviewpress.com. Our print books and ebooks are also available for sale on our site.

On the Broadview website we also offer several goods that are not books—among them the Broadview coffee mug, the Broadview beer stein (inscribed with a line from Geoffrey Chaucer's *Canterbury Tales),* the Broadview fridge magnets (your choice of philosophical or literary), and a range of T-shirts (made from combinations of hemp, bamboo, and/or high-quality pima cotton, with no child labor, sweatshop labor, or environmental degradation involved in their manufacture).

All these goods are available through the "merchandise" section of the Broadview website. When you buy Broadview goods you can support other goods too.

broadview press
www.broadviewpress.com